SOL STEIN S
REFERENCE BOOK FOR WRITERS

ALSO BY SOL STEIN

BOOKS

How to Grow a Novel

Stein on Writing

A Feast for Lawyers

Native Sons (with James Baldwin)

NOVELS

The Husband

The Magician

Living Room

The Childkeeper

Other People

The Resort

The Touch of Treason

A Deniable Man

The Best Revenge

PLAYS

Napoleon (New York and California, 1953)

A Shadow of My Enemy
(National Theater, Washington, D.C., and Broadway, 1957)

SOFTWARE FOR WRITERS

WritePro™

FictionMaster™

FirstAid for Writers®

SOL STEIN'S
REFERENCE BOOK FOR WRITERS

— Sol Stein —

 ST. MARTIN'S GRIFFIN 📖 NEW YORK

SOL STEIN'S REFERENCE BOOK FOR WRITERS. Copyright © 2010 by Sol Stein. All rights reserved. Printed in the United States of America. For information, address St. Martin's Press, 175 Fifth Avenue, New York, N.Y. 10010.

www.stmartins.com

Library of Congress Cataloging-in-Publication Data

Stein, Sol.
    Sol Stein's reference book for writers : part 1: writing, part 2: pulishing / Sol Stein.—1st St. Martin's Griffin ed.
       p. cm.
   ISBN 978-0-312-55095-0 (trade pbk.)
 1. Authorship.   I. Title.
 PN151.S836 2010
 808'.02—dc22

2010032150

First Edition: November 2010

10 9 8 7 6 5 4 3 2 1

DEDICATED WITH LOVE TO THE STEINLINGS

LELAND

ROBIN

DAVID

ELIZABETH

MADELINE

CHARLES

SUMMER GRACE

CONTENTS

PART I: WRITING

Action 1
Action, Physical 1
Adjectives and Adverbs 2
Answering Machine 3
Aphorisms 3
Arias 5
Autobiography 5
Avant-garde 5

Backstory 7
Beginnings, in Crime Novels, Thrillers,
 and Literature 8
Beginnings in Nonfiction and Narrative
 Nonfiction 11
Between Manuscripts 14
Biography 15
Branding by Character 15

Candor 16
Careless Writing 16
Casting a Play 17
Catharsis 18
Chapter Endings 18
Characterization 18
Character Description 20

Character-Driven 21
Character Needs 21
Characterizing Through Actions 21
Characters' Decisions 22
Characters from Life 23
Characters Readers Like 25
Characterization of Inanimate Objects 25
Characters, Perfection of 25
Characters Speaking Other Languages 26
Choosing a Medium—Plays, Film, Fiction 28
   —a Reality Check
Clichés 29
Collaboration 30
Commas 30
Commercial Versus Literary 31
Conflict 32
Continuing Characters 33
Converting Screenplays and Theatrical 33
   Plays into Publishable Fiction
Craft Techniques 35
Creating Emotion in Fiction and Nonfiction 36
Creating Emotion in Film Writing 36
Creating Tension 38
Credibility 39
Criticism, Handling 39
Crucible in Fiction and Nonfiction 40

Detail 41
Developing Drama 42
Dialogue 43
Dialogue, Advanced 45

Diction 47
Drafts 48
Drama 49

Eccentricity 49
Editing and Editors 49
Editing, Need for 50
Editing Nonfiction 52
Editing, Self- 52
Emotion. 53
Ending Chapters. 53
English (the Language) 53
Essays 54
Exercise in Style 55
Expanding Fiction from Within 55
Explication. 56
Exposition 56
An Eye for Detail 57

False Notes 58
Family 58
Fast Writing 58
Fathers (in Fiction and Nonfiction) 58
Faults, Writers' 59
Feedback 60
Fiction, First Three Pages of 61
Fiction, Three Elements of 61
First Appearance (of a Character). 62
First Drafts of Fiction 62
First Paragraphs in Fiction 64
First Readers 65

First Sentences 66
Flab 66
Flashback 67
Flat Characters 67
Flat Writing 67
Fleshing Out 67
Flow 68
Fonts 69
Foreign Words 69
Format for Manuscripts 70
Formula (Stein's) 70
Formulaic Fiction 71
Free Association 71
Fresh Use of Words in Journalism 72
Furniture (in Fiction and Nonfiction) 73

Getting Started 74
Getting Stuck 74
Glitch 75
Grammar Switch 75
Guts 76

Hero and Heroine 76
High Concept 76
Historical Fiction 77
Historical Nonfiction, Responsibility of 77
Hoarding 77
Hooking the Reader 78
How Many Writers Are There? 80
How-to Nonfiction 81

Ideas	83
Immediate Scene	84
Inspiration	84
Interruptions	85
Jargon	87
Journal or Jotting	87
Keeping Track of Different Versions	88
Laziness	89
Learning to Write	90
Legal Issues	90
Line-Editing	91
Line Space	93
Living, Earning a	93
Love Stories or Scenes	94
Mannerism	95
Marker	95
Mark Twain's Rules	96
Melodrama Versus Drama	97
Memoir	99
Metaphors and Similes	100
Minor Characters in Fiction	101
Monologues in Fiction	103
Motivation	103
Multiple Drafts: A Safety Procedure	104
Naming Characters	105
Narration in Fiction	106

Narrative Hook 106
Narrative Nonfiction 107
Narrator.. 108
New Dramatists 108
Newspeak 108
Noise and Interruptions 109
Nonfiction as Literature 110
Notes to Oneself 110
Nothing Happens 111

Observing 111
Opening Scenes in Drama 112
Order of Phrases and Sentences 112
Ordinariness 112
Orwellian 113
Outlining Fiction 114

Page Numbering 114
Paragraph Endings 115
Particularity 115
Planning a Novel 116
Planting 117
Plausibility 117
Playwriting Guidelines 118
Plot 120
Plotting 120
Poetry 122
Point of View 123
Point of View (More) 124
Point of View, Shifting 125
Preaching 125

Precision 125
Precision and Freshness in Public Speaking. 126
Prologues 127
Punctuation 128

Readers 128
Reading 129
Reading for Screenwriters 129
Reading Other Writers 129
Realism and Fantasy in Drama 130
Realism in Fiction 130
Real People in Fiction 130
Rebirth of Abandoned Manuscripts 131
Recommended Reading for Writers 132
Repetition 135
Resonance 136
Revision 137

Scene 140
Scene Inspiration and Instruction 140
Screenplay Technique in Fiction 141
Screenwriting 142
Segue 143
Self-Confidence 143
Senses 144
Sentence Length 144
Sentimentality 145
Settings 146
Sex Scenes 147
Short Advice from the Masters Amended 148
"Show, Don't Tell" in Fiction 148

"Show, Don't Tell" in Nonfiction 148
Showing and Telling 149
Simple Character Solutions 149
Slang 150
Social Class in Fiction 151
Social Class in Nonfiction 151
Sounds Wrong 151
Stein's Prescriptions 152
Stereotypes 153
Story Progression 153
Straying 153
Stream of Consciousness 154
Strength (in Writing) 154
Stressing the Reader 154
Strong Characters 154
Stuck? 155
Style 155
Subject Matter 156
Surprises 156
Suspense in Fiction 156
Suspense in Nonfiction 157
Synopsis 158

Talking Shop with Other Writers 159
Telegraphing 159
Telephone Answering 159
Telling 160
Tense 160
Tension 161
Theme 163
Time Away from a Draft 164

Time to Write 164
Titles 165
Training 169
Treasure 169
Typeface Recommendation 170

Uncertainty When Beginning Fiction 171
Usage 172

Verbs 172
Verisimilitude 172
Villains 173
Visualization 173

Weekends 175
What the Reader Wants 176
What to Write? 177
What Your Book Is About (Fiction and Nonfiction) 177
When Is a Manuscript Ready to Be Sent to an
 Agent or a Publisher? 178
When to Write 179
Where to Start If You're Writing Fiction 179
Where to Write 179
Why Readers Read Fiction 180
Why Write? 180
Working Habits 180
Working Hours 181
Writerly 181
Writer's Block 182
Writer's Courage 183
Writing About Faces 183

Writing as an Obsession 184
Writing as a Profession 185
Writing Workshops 187

You 188
Your Assets as Liabilities in Character Creation 189

PART 2: PUBLISHING

Acquiring Editors 190
Advance or Royalty Advance (Payment Received from a Publisher) 191
Agents 191

Backlist 193
Biggest Changes in Publishing as a Business 193
Book Advertising 195
Book Banning 196
Book Clubs 196
Book Clubs for Reading Groups 197
Book Manufacturing 197
Bookselling 198
Bookselling on Consignment 199
Book Tours 200
Bound Galleys 201
Byline 202

Categories of Fiction 202
Chain Stores 203
Children's Books and Young Adult Books 204
Choosing Subjects for Nonfiction 204

Commercial 205
Commissioned Nonfiction 205
Commissioning Fiction 206
Competition 206
Contracts, Book 207
Contractual Issues 209
Controversial Content 210
Copyediting 210

Deadline 211
Deep Discount 211
Delivery Date 212
Delivery Option for Manuscripts 213
Direct Mail 213
Direct Marketing 214

Editing 214
Editorial Boards 216
Editor's Functions 217
Electronic Rights 218

Fair Use 219
First Serial Rights 219
Foreign Sales, Fiction 219
Foreign Sales, Nonfiction 221
Format for Manuscripts 221
Freelance Editors 223

Genre 224

Handle 224

Interview Tips 225
Inventory 226

Jacket Copy 227

Keeping in Touch 228
Kill Fee 228

Lecturing 229
Legal Issues 230
Letters 230
Library Sales 231
Life After Death: An Insider's Tale 232
Location 234

Management 234
Marketing Timetable 235
Mass-Market Books 235
Midlist 235
Multiple Queries 237
Multiple Submissions 237

Nature of the Publishing Business 238
Nonfiction, Commissioned 238

Option 238

Packagers 239
Pen Names 240
Press Kits and Presentation Folders 241

Prestige 242
Proposals 242
Publicity and Promotion 243
Publicity, the Writer's Role 246
Publishing Is a Business 248

Quality Paperbacks 250

Remainders 251
Returning Advances 252
Returns 252
Review Quotes 252
Reviving Authors 253
Royalties 254

Sales Meetings 255
Seasons in Publishing 257
Self-Publishing 257
Stunts Sell Books 258
Subsidiary Rights 259

Track Records 259

Unearned Advances 260

Value of Books 261

Warning to New Senior Executives 262
Writers' Rights 262

I AM GRATEFUL FOR HIS GUIDANCE TO

GEORGE WITTE,

AN EDITOR WHO EDITS EDITORS WITH

EXPERIENCE, KNOWLEDGE, AND TACT.

INTRODUCTION

The A–Z "Writing" section is primarily for writers of fiction, nonfiction, narrative nonfiction, film, theater, and essays. Its main purpose is to provide help *quickly* to a writer in need of particular help while writing, and to maintain momentum by encouraging immediate return to a manuscript in progress. I expect that some editors and other publishing personnel may peek in to see what writers think about. Similarly, writers needing to understand publishing terms and processes can at leisure examine related matters in the "Publishing" section of this book.

Much can be learned from specialties other than one's own. A participant in one of my seminars was the author of more than thirty nonfiction books, who picked up pointers originally designed for fiction writers. The Fiction Weekends that I gave for a number of years surprised me by attracting novelists who at the time already had books on the bestseller list but were happy to join less experienced hopefuls because the learning process for a serious writer does not end with publication. One improves craft throughout a writing lifetime.

—Sol Stein

PART 1: WRITING

A

Action

An action in fiction is a forward movement of the story that doesn't necessarily involve physical activity. In fiction a surprising or strongly worded or decisive thought can be an action. For instance, if the leading character decides she must investigate something—why a door that is always kept closed is open or why her husband is coming home later and later—those thoughts are actions. Action can be slamming a door, refusing to make a loan, moving a crucial chess piece, going somewhere unexpected, anything that involves *significant change*. Inaction is static. For instance, a scene with two characters chatting agreeably but not disagreeing about anything important is inactive and does not propel a story forward. To make conversation active, see **Dialogue**.

Action, Physical

The key in story writing is plausibility. This statement is not propaganda for realism, it means simply that any action needs to be sufficiently credible so the reader won't stop and think *this sounds made-up*. In thrillers and suspense novels, the most common mistakes occur when the hero or villain does things that are unlikely in life. For instance, I once edited a popular author who had one character throw another character over a ship's railing. Can we believe that one character is strong enough to raise another person high enough to throw him over a railing? Even if that is possible, for the reader it is not easily credible. An action must be instantly believable. Do characters in novels do out-of-the-ordinary things? Yes. But they are done credibly. An author can make a reader see, feel, hear, smell, and believe. Physical exaggerations work against belief.

Children's books frequently have implausible action set in an environment created by the writer in which such things become possible. The possibility has to be established early. Science fiction, when well wrought, does the same thing. In literary fiction a writer might stray unnecessarily, for example by having a young leading lady crying so copiously that her dress gets wet. Not likely. Therefore, the attempt becomes a glitch in the reader's experience (see **Glitch**).

Adjectives and Adverbs
These weaken nouns and verbs, and therefore weaken your writing. For instance, "Life is great" is a strong statement. "Life is frequently great" is much weaker, though it may be more accurate under the circumstances. In general, I advise care in the use of adjectives and adverbs. At times they are needed for accuracy and comprehension. In speech, adjectives and adverbs are commonplace, habitual, and often unnecessary. Overuse of adjectives in speaking can sap the strength of prose. That's where we get the habit. This morning's edition of my favorite newspaper has a lead editorial about protecting "Americans' cherished rights." "Cherished rights" is weaker than "Americans' rights" because of the cliché adjec-

tive. If the writer was desperate for an adjective—though none was needed—he or she could have weakened the noun less by choosing a less familiar adjective. If you must have an adjective, use an unusual one. When revising writing, one should develop the habit of checking for and cutting unneeded adjectives and adverbs to strengthen prose. See **Clichés**.

Answering Machine

If you are like most writers, a phone ringing in the midst of writing can disrupt the flow of thought. Answering machines are only a partial remedy because the ringing of the phone can itself do the harm. One solution is to have phones at more than one location, one in some other room or place that rings and takes your messages and in your writing room another phone that doesn't have a ringer or that has a ringer that can be silenced when not wanted. If you're concerned about emergency calls, tell your family to call twice in a row if one really needs to disturb your work. You can probably think of other solutions that fit your circumstances better. The main point is to avoid interruptions.

Aphorisms

Sometimes called an adage or a maxim, an aphorism is a brief truism or cleverly stated perception. An aphorism is usually welcomed by readers in dialogue if it is spoken appropriately by a fictional character and is consistent with what's happening at that point in the story. *An aphorism should not draw attention to itself while the reader is reading.* A novelist can make good use of aphorisms if they are spoken by the right characters in appropriate circumstances. I scrounged through a novel of mine, *The Best Revenge,* and found the following examples of aphorisms used by characters in the novel:

"Of course the Bible was written by sinners. How else would they know?"

"Experience is what enables you to have a guilty conscience when you do something you know is wrong because you've done it before."

"The best way to move is like a duck, calm on the surface, paddling like hell underneath."

"The important creases are in the brain, not in the pants."

"I remembered the expression Bette Davis had in a movie when she was saying yes like she was surrendering a country."

"The truth is people take hostages. Sometimes the hostages they take are themselves."

"My accountant is an owl of a man who keeps one eyelid half shut not because of an affliction but because there is much in this world he is not prepared to see."

"Show business is a hill of ice, and when you're on top all you see are the little figures climbing up toward you with pickaxes."

"Save your breath. It's the Devil who negotiates. God never made a deal with nobody."

"There is a kind of thought that sticks in your head the way a piece of chewing gum can stick to the sole of your shoe. The more you try to get rid of it, the worse it seems to get."

"A lawyer is a soldier. His job is to go out and kill the

enemy. You wind him up, point him in the right direction, and get the hell out of the way. All the rest is bullshit."

"If you push the first domino, you are responsible for all that fall."

"A good teacher leaves his tattoo on your brain."

"If you want to understand a people, listen to their special words. In Yiddish, *naches* means the pride a parent gets from the achievements of a child. Who else gives their kids such a need to provide *naches* to their parents?"

Arias

Wonderful in operas, can be deadly in plays. I may have coined the word "speechifying" because one character going on and on can be as boring onstage as he would be in life. Dialogue can be defined as a verbal clash between two or more characters. Of course, theater has had some significant and brilliant monologues that require great skill to write and hold an audience, but the majority of plays play best when two characters thrust and parry with words. See **Dialogue.**

Autobiography

A book-length author's view of his or her own life, usually told in full if not in full disclosure. It differs from a memoir, which has selected portions of a life.

Avant-garde

A term related to "advanced" or experimental literature, usually fiction. Early in the twentieth century James Joyce's masterpiece *Ulysses* demonstrated how various moments of time relate to each other. His characters' feelings are evoked by memories seeping into consciousness, juxtaposing inner time to clock time by the fluid lapping of the stream of consciousness against the present moment. This kind of feeling predominated in the works of major writers like Proust and Virginia Woolf as well as Joyce. The chief characters in *Ulysses* are Leopold Bloom; his wife, Molly; and Stephen Dedalus, a young man often interpreted to be Joyce himself. It was a time when Freud and psychoanalysis influenced the intelligentsia. Writers wanted to experiment in their stories with the stream of consciousness uncensored, intermixed with memories, providing readers with a new form of storytelling that depended on the interior monologues of the main characters. In *Ulysses* the experienced reader enjoyed the meanderings of Bloom's and Stephen's consciousness and Molly's climactic monologue.

Joyce's next book, *Finnegans Wake,* strayed even further from the literary conventions of the time and seemed incomprehensible to many, with the last page segueing into the first page. I confess that at Columbia University I used to read small parts of *Finnegans Wake* aloud to groups in an Irish accent, which made much of what was happening intelligible to listeners for the first time. The best way to familiarize yourself with Joyce's work is to start with *Dubliners,* his short stories, and his early book, *A Portrait of the Artist as a Young Man.*

B

Backstory

In fiction or narrative nonfiction, events or scenes that happened earlier are called "backstory." Such past scenes are designed to cast light on current events, enriching them. Backstories are most effective when they are visible scenes from the past, not mere summaries. Segueing smoothly into and out of backstory without disrupting the reader's experience is a difficult craft that requires experience, experiment, and practice. When mastered it can be useful to both fiction and nonfiction writers. Moreover, the move to backstory can be accomplished with a change to a different character's point of view, as in the following example:

In my novel *The Best Revenge,* the principal character is Ben Riller, a Broadway producer. In chapter 3, experienced from Riller's point of view, he is having a stormy first meeting with Nick Manucci, a big-time loan shark who Riller knew as a boy. At the end of chapter 3, the protagonist Ben Riller seems to have been bested by Manucci in their meeting. Chapter 4 switches to Manucci's point of view, with an angry and caustic backstory of his growing up and his difficult relationship to his father, from whom he learned the moneylending business. In the reading, the segue is invisible. It doesn't seem abrupt, and the reader experiences the backstory, only to have chapter 5 be yet another backstory, this one from the point of view of Mary Manucci, the wife of the loan shark, revealing the story of her marriage.

Chapter 6 is back in the voice of Nick, the loan shark, in the critical scene with Ben Riller that was interrupted by *two whole chapters of backstory*. The only external reference from author to reader is the chapter titles, which are simply the name of the character speaking. In other words, I used two backstories to interrupt and strengthen the main conflict in the novel. I was pleased to find that readers did not notice that the novel segued into the points of view of other characters in the middle of a tense argument.

The principle to be observed is that one can segue into the past unnoticeably, even to the extent of two chapters, and slip back into the present without the reader noticing and without breaking the continuity of the reader's experience.

Beginnings, in Crime Novels, Thrillers, and Literature

The differences are great. In crime novels, a body is found early, often on page 1. In thrillers an emergency, local, national, or international, is often threatened, unveiled, or begun in the first pages. In literary fiction, the specific manner of beginning a novel may differ significantly from writer to writer.

Henry James remembered Ivan Turgenev saying that his story almost always began with the vision of one or more characters hovering before him, soliciting him, appealing to him, becoming vivid to him, at which point Turgenev imagined and invented and selected and pieced together the situations most useful to his sense of the creatures themselves, the complications they would most likely produce. To arrive at these things, Turgenev said, was to arrive at his story. "If I watch them long enough I see them engaged in this or that act and in this or that difficulty. How they look and move and speak and behave in the setting I have found for them."

In fiction, there are two ways of trying to entice the reader to nestle down in his or her chair for the ride. In commercial thrillers, a killing is about to happen, or a bomb is set to go off. I'm seldom attracted to such stories unless I am first attracted to one or more of the people involved, including the corpse. Many writers have heard me say the reader must know the people in the car before he sees the car crash.

The first few sentences of a novel are the perfect place to involve the reader with a character. (See **Characterization**.) This isn't a new idea. Herman Melville learned this in the nineteenth century, when he started to write a novel badly:

> *It was the middle of a bright tropical afternoon that we made good our escape from the bay. The vessel we sought lay with her main-topsail aback about a league from the land and was the only object that broke the broad expanse of the ocean.*

So what? First there's that word "escape." From what? From land to the ocean? Do we care? We don't have any sense of who is talking. It's an inadequate beginning. Let's look at Melville's later draft of the beginning of the same book:

> *Call me Ishmael. Some years ago—never mind how long precisely—having little or no money in my purse, and nothing particular to interest me on shore, I thought I would sail about a little and see the watery part of the world.*

Those first three words—"Call me Ishmael"—are, of course, the beginning of an acknowledged masterpiece, *Moby-Dick,* and the reader's curiosity is born. Who is this Ishmael with the strong voice who instructs us? A character pulls us into the story.

Writing a beginning that starts with a particular character is also suitable for a commercial crime novel, where the body is found on page 1. Starting with the character who finds the body is better than starting with the body.

In novels that aspire to be literature, starting with a character at an event will produce a stronger beginning than starting with the event. One of the very best is the beginning of *Rabbit at Rest*, the fourth volume of John Updike's Rabbit series. Updike uses the first paragraph to reintroduce the protagonist Rabbit Angstrom and provides the reader with a dramatic setting and two conflicts, neither of which Rabbit can control. It's an ideal beginning.

> *Standing amid the tan, excited post-Christmas crowd at the Southwest Florida Regional Airport, Rabbit Angstrom has a funny feeling that what he has come to meet, what's floating in unseen about to land, is not his son Nelson and daughter-in-law Pru and their two children but something more ominous and intimately his: his own death, shaped vaguely like an airplane. The sensation chills him, above and beyond the terminal air-conditioning. But, then, facing Nelson has made him feel uneasy for thirty years.*

A common fault in beginnings—and elsewhere—is to provide the reader information about the birth or early years of a character unrelated to the story. Here's a rare case of relevance:

> *Ambrose was born in the Woman's Detention Center on Rikers Island. Normally a pregnant prisoner would be transferred to a se-*

cure facility at a hospital shortly before she was due to deliver but Ambrose was born ahead of schedule without much warning. Ambrose always got a headache when he had to fill out a questionnaire that asked for his place of birth.

It is also possible to introduce an important character through his thoughts. Chapter 1 of my novel *The Touch of Treason* introduces the leading character, George Thomassy, this way:

In the end you died. There could be a courtroom like this, Thomassy thought; all the good wood bleached white, the judge deaf to objections because He owned the place. The law was His, the advocacy system finished.

If that's what it was going to be like, George Thomassy wanted to live forever because here on earth, God willing or not, you could fight back.

Beginnings in Nonfiction and Narrative Nonfiction

If yours is a practical book about the use of screws in homemade furniture, the interested reader will buy it for its information. We're talking about nonfiction books that need to attract and hold readers: histories, biographies, books about politics, international relations, psychology, and many other subjects, as well as narrative nonfiction. Many writers of such books have used techniques developed in fiction for involving readers immediately. The fact that you are writing nonfiction is no excuse for boring your reader.

A friend of mine, Donald Passman, is the author of a nonfiction book entitled *All You Need to Know About the Music Business*. The book is a standard in its field. You would imagine that a book of instruction and definition might be dry. Not this one. Passman doesn't even wait for page 1 to attract the reader. After the title page there is a page headlined "Did You Know That . . ." It goes on like this:

• *Most record deals don't require the record company even to make a record, much less release it?*

• *The term "phonograph record" in recording contracts included home video devices at least ten years before these devices even existed.*

And so on, surprising facts that are amusing to read. His acknowledgments page is also amusing. His first page of text has this heading: "OPEN UP AND SAY 'AHHH,'" as if the author were a dentist. The book itself contains serious information and instruction in a complex field, *but you expect to enjoy reading it.* Is it any wonder that the book has had at least four editions and that the author later got a huge advance for his first novel?

Barnaby Conrad, a prodigious creator of at least twenty books and thirteen grandchildren, seems to think I am an authority on beginnings of stories, novels, and plays. I may surprise him by suggesting that similar techniques are also available to the writer of nonfiction and narrative. For instance, in 1989 I wrote a nonfiction book called *A Feast for Lawyers* for which I wanted a grabber of an opening, so I entitled the first chapter "An Open Letter to the Congress of the United States," which aroused the curiosity of quite a few influential people. Wait. To ensure my hold on the reader, the first sentence read, "At this writing, two scandals have been robbing Americans of more money than all the thieves of the last two centuries put together: the Savings & Loan scandal and the Chapter 11 scandal."

I am a true believer in the importance of having an enticing opening for nonfiction as well as for novels and stories. What you've just read is an available technique of making a statement that many readers may instantly challenge and want the author to prove. Start with a challenge. Other readers may be attracted to the disclosure of large-scale villainy, and take to the book with an "at last" feeling.

Biography and autobiography cry out for interesting writing rather than a recital of facts from the past. Elia Kazan called his autobiography simply *A Life*. If you were in a bookstore and you didn't know who Kazan was or weren't interested in the only American to reach the top in directing film and theater and also to have a record-breaking thirty-seven-week hold on the number 1 spot on the *New York Times* bestseller list in fiction, your curiosity might just get you to look at page 1. Here is his first paragraph of autobiography:

> "Why are you mad?" My wife asks me that; seems like every morning. Usually at breakfast, when my face is still wrinkled from sleep. "I'm not mad," I say. "It's just my face." I've said that to her ten times. She's my third wife and I'm happy with her, but she has yet to learn that I don't like to talk in the morning. Which is tough on her, a decent person, full of lively chatter like bright pebbles.

Note how Kazan in a few lines involves the reader in wanting to know more about the writer and his wife, who are onstage and interacting. And note the writerly ending of that first paragraph, "like bright pebbles."

Wil Haygood's biography of Sammy Davis Jr., *In Black and White,* displays a different technique for capturing the reader. Note how the author *ends* the first paragraph on page 1:

> There are many from the 1940s and 1950s who watched him grow up—onstage—and feel a kind of surrogate connection with him. His name often drops warmly from their lips. Like kin.
> Sammy.

The "like kin" warms the reader. And the second paragraph is just one word: "Sammy," and brings the subject and the reader closer. It's a marvelous way of drawing the reader into a life.

Between Manuscripts

Vacation travel between novels is fine. Take a slim pad that can slide into any garment, even a bathrobe with pockets. If you get a fleeting idea, write it down—don't rely on memory. If you're into a novel and vacation time comes around, do the same; a writer can't—or shouldn't—empty his mind for any reason. Based on my experience, the longer your career, the more apt you will be to have random aperçus or thoughts that seem like little gems. You are never wholly relieved of the task of noting something fresh, an idea, a person, a situation, and it's all to the good.

Warning: There comes a time when you put a manuscript into the hands of your agent or editor and the world seems to have stopped spinning. Life becomes suspended animation.

Days seem like weeks. You're stuck in a desert and an oasis is hard to find. Your recipient is not inconsiderate; he hasn't turned against you; he is a busy person, an editor or agent of many authors, and quite possibly has a family and other obligations. Start a new manuscript. First refresh yourself by reading the characterization entries in this book. Write one paragraph. Rewrite it. Does it have resonance? Does it sing? Would I want to read the next paragraph? You will have made constructive use of your waiting time. Congratulations on your maturity as a writer!

Biography
The recounting of a life told by someone other than the subject. If you consider yourself an intellectual, I would greatly commend to you Michael Ignatieff's biography *Isaiah Berlin: A Life,* a grand though overlooked book about a highly influential twentieth-century philosopher who was much admired by Churchill, had a college at Oxford established in his honor, spoke his thoughts, and luckily had a talented writer as a nearby friend. Warning: If your ambition is to write a great biography, you will find this one intimidating.

Branding by Character
Sherlock Holmes was the character and the brand. A new Sherlock Holmes book might appeal to any reader who had read a previous Sherlock Holmes book. I used to look down on the process of branding by character but my readers taught me to use the George Thomassy character again. I now have several novels that are quite different from each other except

for the fact that the lawyer Thomassy appears in them, and as is his wont, he manages to take over whichever stage he is on. Branding by character works in both commercial and literary genres.

C

Candor

Candor is essential in writing. A serious writer of fiction not only conveys external life, but also writes what his characters think. Frankness in writing, openness, honesty, and truthfulness heighten the effect of both nonfiction and fiction. The freshness of a candid revelation—even if it is inadvertent—by a character in a play or novel can make a scene stand out. Candor in writing should be appropriate and accurate in the circumstances conveyed. I remember a mature writing student in a seminar whose country-club writing did not interest the other members of the seminar. When he understood the effectiveness of candor, he created a chapter in which a priest is delivering a sermon while his underpants are slipping and he is trying to avoid looking at a female parishioner he finds attractive. It worked.

Careless Writing

I have often referred to this as "top-of-the-head" writing, meaning letting the sentences flow without care, a kind of near-automatic writing typical of some commercial writers whose lawyers won't let me use their names with impunity. A writer is and should be judged by the carefulness, freshness, and accuracy of the words he uses. This requires thought. It's quite fair for a writer to say, "How do I know what I think until I see what I say?" Careless writing is typing whatever first comes to mind. The writer concerned with reputation as well as remuneration examines his work either immediately or later, but should take the time to judge what he has written for accuracy, freshness, and melody. That means to be sure of the correctness of what he's written, its originality when possible, and whether in context its rhythm sings.

Casting a Play

This is the director's provenance but the writer should be present as a watchdog for actors whose physical appearance could hurt a play. This sounds like a small point but it had enormous consequences in one of my plays in 1957. The first locale was Ford's Theater in Baltimore, where segregation was still in force. The cast was booked into a nearby hotel, but the single black actress was not permitted to register. She had to stay at a hotel some distance from the theater. The director wanted her to at least have some company in the off-hours. He hired a black male actor to play the small part of an FBI man who testified briefly in a court scene. The idea was noble, but in practice was awful because the black FBI man threw an unscripted puzzle into what was intended to be a tense moment in the play. A white midget or a seven-foot-high white person would have had the same unwanted effect, focusing the audience's concentration on size. The writer's work is at risk during the casting process, and the writer should be on the lookout for casting that would be wrong for the part. In that same play, the leading actor could not pronounce the name of the mountain Kathmandu. As a result a very important speech had to be eliminated.

Catharsis

In writing novels the author is playing on the emotions of the reader. In emotional climaxes within or at the end of a novel, the reader should be experiencing emotional relief, hence a catharsis. Well-crafted short stories can produce the same satisfying effect.

Chapter Endings

The goal is to compel the reader to begin the next chapter. This is especially important in the early chapters of a novel. A *satisfying* conclusion to a scene will not thrust the reader into the next chapter. Something new—a development, a problem, a turn in fortune, a surprise—compels the reader to turn to the next chapter. If the reader is anxious to see a certain door opened, don't open the door at the beginning of the next chapter. Go somewhere else, leaving the reader in suspense. A new chapter is sometimes a good place for a backstory episode to begin. The main point is to continue and sustain the suspense. A rule to consider for the following chapter is "Never take the reader where the reader wants to go."

Characterization

Do you remember Sherlock Holmes or do you remember the plots? When you think of the movies you've seen in years past, do you remember the characters or plot details? Long ago, a book entitled *Characters Make Your Story* was published. You don't need to read the book; the title tells it all. When beginning a work of fiction a writer might think, *How will I interest the reader?* The literary writer will want the reader to fall in love with her character. The plot-oriented writer might think how to hook the reader. A hook is plot oriented. One would do well to remember that Sherlock Holmes was not a particularly nice guy, he was a dope addict and treated Dr. Watson badly, but it was the characterization that lured you into the story. Note that writers of popular series mysteries use their ongoing character to entice the reader. The emphasis on characterization works for both literary and commercial fiction.

If you like rules, pick one from life. People who interest you are usually individuals who are in some way different from everyone else you know. A character with special strength for dealing with large problems is far more interesting than a hesitant character drowning in his own inadequacies.

Here are a few ways to help you characterize when writing fiction, plays, and screenplays.

> 1. An imperfection can help make something seem real: a visible spot on a tie, muddy shoe tracks, food that has lumps, water that is not quite clear, ungrammatical speech, a baby that won't smile however hard a mother tries to engage it.
>
> 2. Abruptness in speech, as in, "No. I said no. I meant no."
>
> 3. Repetitiveness. "She straightened the napkin on her lap, but it wasn't to her satisfaction so she straightened it again and a third time so that finally everybody at the table was watching her."

4. Make descriptions of places a bit unusual: "Their living room was like a little railroad station, family members coming in and out seemingly without purpose but in a hurry, an occasional shout from somewhere upstairs to someone elsewhere in the house, a sense that without this activity everybody would be instantly dead."

5. Personality flaws shown through dialogue: "I don't know why I don't believe her; it's just that voice of hers makes even small talk seem hysterical."

Character Description

Warning: A laundry list of character traits does not necessarily bring a character to life. A favorite example of mine concerns a character named Murray. If I write, "Murray was haunted by his past," that isn't really effective. If, however, I write, "When speaking to people, Murray's hand moved to his open collar as if searching for the tie he used to wear," I am signaling that Murray is old enough to have once had the habit of wearing a tie.

A favorite technique of mine is to have one character describe another in a way that characterizes both at the same time. I also use the technique for generating a bit of conflict right at the outset. For example I have a character named Archibald Widmer saying about the protagonist,

> *Of course a man like George Thomassy puts me on edge. His voice is devoid of civility, it reaches out to you as if it were a command. He laughs too loud. I've seen him bite off a hangnail in public. If he agrees with anything you say, he winks one eye as if expressing approval to a child. I rarely met his type socially before he became involved with my daughter. Francine is not the only woman who*

believes Thomassy looks like Robert Redford, but I can't see the resemblance for the life of me. It may have been a monumental blunder for me to introduce Francine to Thomassy at a time when her life was at risk."

See **Social Class in Fiction.**

Character-Driven

A term used by fiction writers, their agents, and editors. Stories and novels are spoken of as plot-driven or character-driven. Plot-driven stories strive for suspense. Character-driven fiction is also suspenseful (it better be!), but the concentration is on the living people created by the author. See **Social Class in Fiction.**

Character Needs

A character without needs is dead. Needs characterize a person quickly. Needs can also kick-start a plot.

Characterizing Through Actions

When we encounter people in daily life we usually notice first how they look. On occasion we will notice a person's action before seeing what he or she looks like, but when writing the temptation is to first describe how a character looks. Sometimes it will benefit a story to introduce a character by his or her action if the action is unusual, striking, and significant. Especially significant. Here's an example of a principal character's action that is important to the book:

> *Henry was unusual even as a child. If in the schoolyard two other eight-year-olds were pushing each other's chests, threatening each other, yelling preparatory to fisticuffs in the schoolyard, Henry would step between them—a dangerous place to be sometimes—and elicit from each the reason for their hostility. He might be told it was none of his business, but Henry had a reputation for making the conflicts of others his business. Henry insisted on getting from each party the reason for their hostility, which when elicited often sounded so trivial that the peacemaker could rapidly tone down the verbal venom, which added to Henry's reputation as a peacemaker.*

From Henry's action we get an early sniff of plot, what Henry's hazardous life might become.

Tip: Readers prefer *active* characters.

Characters' Decisions

I've repeatedly warned that a fiction writer's job is to create emotions in the reader. We can take "Don't tell, show!" a step further, "showing" a character coming to a decision through an unrelated action. For instance, if an important decision is to be made, the reader can feel it through the character's involvement with, say, an object. Here's an example from *How to Grow a Novel:*

> *Early the next morning, as Amory headed for the garage, his special oak tree, the one that marked the end of the lawn, let go of a leaf. It drifted one way, then the other, losing altitude, wafting like a slow pendulum till it settled, brown and intact, on the pebbles at his feet. He stooped to pick it up by the stem. Against the early morning light, he could see every vein of its astounding symmetry. As he laid it carefully on his left palm, wondering what to do with it, the dry leaf fractured into crumbles, its shape vanished. He let the remains*

drop to the hard ground. For an insane second he wanted to stoop and salvage one piece of it to put in his wallet.

He looked up. The oak had plenty of leaves left. He got into his car and zoomed out of the driveway, headed for the great restorer, work.

Characters from Life

If you've lived long enough to be able to use this book for your writing, you have met men, women, and children who have eccentricities worth thinking about when peopling a story. For instance, a long time ago I ran an upscale book club called the Mid-Century Book Society, and the judges who made the final decisions on main selections were a distinguished group, Jacques Barzun, Lionel Trilling, and W. H. Auden. We were all shareholders and therefore required to attend an occasional meeting in the offices of Arnold Bernhard, who had financed the venture. Bernhard's formal boardroom had a huge mural on one wall reminiscent of the kind of art that was popular in the early 1930s Works Progress Administration. Auden was the most eccentric of our group and obviously didn't enjoy formal board meetings, so he would arrive with his tie around the outside of his collar and slippers instead of shoes on his feet. He looked—and maybe felt—like a free man prepared to be comfortable while bored. Auden also used to throw birthday parties for himself at home, offering champagne (cooled among ice cubes in his bathtub) and ordinary white bread, which he said was very good for soaking up alcohol. And so when I think of new characters for fiction, I think of Auden's eccentricities of dress and party-giving and then riffle through my memory for other eccentricities my characters can use.

Children are often portrayed without any special characteristics or doing something usual like bouncing a ball. One of my granddaughters was a bit of a gymnast by the age of four. When we took her along to a sophisticated Portuguese restaurant, she immediately noticed the round brass railing along the raised area where we sat and on her own initiative performed her gymnastics on the railing while we adults ate. Eventually she seemed to be entertaining everyone in the restaurant who could see her. Think of eccentricity you've observed and how you might use it in your work.

Several writers of commercial fiction use characters that exist in real life or did in the historical period of the novel. I know a successful thriller writer whose breakthrough into big-league commercial fiction came when he put a couple of very well-known contemporaries (contemporary in the time of the novel) into his work. Another writer, Joseph Kanon, whose first novel, *Los Alamos,* was well received by reviewers and readers, used J. Robert Oppenheimer, the physicist who headed the Manhattan Project and whose mission was to build the first atomic bomb. In the novel, several historical characters have small roles but Oppenheimer is an important character. One caution: It's best to use public personages who are no longer with us. While most famous people won't sue if their namesake in a novel does horrendous things or is ugly, one doesn't want to chance lawsuits. Unless, of course, the writer is seeking a public brouhaha that will provide publicity for his book! Also beware of using real restaurants or other businesses if the context is negative.

Characters Readers Like
My friend Barnaby Conrad knows more facets of writing craft than anyone I've known and admired. He emphasizes that readers like to read about people who *are good at what they do.* I learned that truth with a character named George Thomassy, a lawyer who turned out to be the most memorable character of my novel *The Magician.* The protagonist is supposed to be the sixteen-year-old magician, but readers seem to have bonded with Thomassy through his courtroom performances. The Thomassy character has followed me into several other novels and has been the main cause of two movie deals because actors want to play him as much as readers want to read about him. My advice is let a successful character make his way into other writings if appropriate. Also remember that readers tend to like characters that are *good at what they do.*

Characterization of Inanimate Objects
In books designed to be read by adults, we need to be careful not to overdo this kind of characterization, but occasionally such characterization can contribute to the pleasure of reading. For instance, a sad tricycle standing in a corner of the room, concerned that it was taking so long to turn into a bicycle.

Characters, Perfection of
In Robert Frost's "A Masque of Reason" God says to Job,

> *Society can never think things out:*
> *It has to see them acted out by actors,*
> *Devoted actors at a sacrifice—*
> *The ablest actors I can lay my hands on.*

This sage advice was not passed on to me by Robert Frost but by Bertram Wolfe, an author of several important books it was my privilege to edit. Brooklyn-born Wolfe knew personally some of the great villains in the twentieth century, including Stalin and his cohorts. Wolfe knew as close friends some of the great artists of his time, Diego Rivera and Frida Kahlo. Wolfe's book *The Fabulous Life of Diego Rivera* won the National Book Award. Reading even a few of its pages will benefit any writer with literary aspirations.

Characters Speaking Other Languages
Bad cowboy stories of another era sometimes had an American Indian saying things like "Me good Indian, him bad cowboy." The adult reader of fiction in the twenty-first century requires writing that is not a caricature of spoken language. For illustrative purposes, I am assuming the writer is using English but is creating a character for which English is not a native language and is spoken imperfectly. For convenience, I've chosen an example from my novel *The Best Revenge,* in which three members of the Manucci family are important to the story. Nick Manucci is American-born and speaks normal English. So does his wife, Mary Manucci. However, Mike's father, Aldo Manucci, an important character early in the story, speaks English as an immigrant might. The old man is brought into the reader's presence by a young woman. The elder Manucci has a visitor, Ben Riller, a Broadway play producer who grew up in the East Bronx and whose father was a friend of old man Manucci. Note Manucci's use of an invented language and how it is introduced gradually.

At last she wheeled him in, a shrunken human stuffed by a careless taxidermist. He was trying to hold his head up to see me, an eye clouded by cataract. He took an unblinking look, then let a rich smile lift the ends of his mouth as his voice, still bass though tremulous, said, "Ben-neh!" which made my name sound like the word "good" in Italian.

"Mr. Manucci," I said, and took his hand in both of mine, which were cold. His hand was warm, for he had long ago abjured nervousness about anything that life might bring him.

"You a much big man now," Manucci said. "In papers all time Ben-neh Riller present, Ben-neh Riller announce, Ben-neh Riller big stars, big shows. You bring Gina Lollobrigida here I kiss her hand. I kiss her anything," he laughed. "Magnani, you know Magnani, she more my type. I tell people here I know you when you just a little Jew kid this high." He held his hand up flat to show my height when he saw me last. "Your father, Louie, he just a shrimp, how you get so big? Oh this my niece, Clara. I call her Clarissima, she best woman ever in my life."

First, Aldo Manucci is set up as a fragile old man in a wheelchair who still has power behind his voice. Manucci's Italian is set up with the name of a character that is familiar to the reader as Ben, for which Manucci uses an Italianate diminutive, Ben-neh. Manucci leaves out verbs, as in "she more my type," "I know you when you just a little Jew kid this high," "she best woman ever in my life."

When Ben asks the old man for the loan of a large sum of money, Manucci says, "How much you need." When he hears the amount, he whistles and says, "Ho boy," instead of the usual "Oh boy."

Choosing a Medium—Plays, Film, Fiction—a Reality Check

This is a brief overview of a complex subject, directed here to the beginning writer or to a writer questioning the medium he is working in. I share my experience in each.

Writing plays for productions with professional actors for paying audiences can be a joyous experience but an uncertain way of making a living. You need a strong talent for dialogue. You subsidize your own writing, if you're lucky you'll get a small advance on acceptance by a producer, and from that point on you rely mainly on other people, actors, a director, a producer, for the success of your writing enterprise. Monitoring rehearsals for weeks is a tough assignment, especially in out-of-town tryouts, often with quick script changes needing to be written overnight before copies are made.

Writing screenplays is an even tougher occupation. It requires a strong visual talent in addition to skill in dialogue writing. Even more than theater, screenplays are a communal enterprise. The producer and director and sometimes even leading actors will suggest changes in the script. The glamour attached to film tempts many would-be screenwriters; it has been said that in the Los Angeles area alone some fifty thousand people list their occupation as "screenwriter," though only one will place a script during a year. Of course there are professionals who have succeeded with screenplays who keep getting new assignments or fashion their own and become "names" in the industry. It is appropriate to wonder why so many well-known writers in other fields fled Hollywood because of its strange, arrogant, and sometimes debilitating culture. If you're heading for the screen, nothing will stop you. The pay is good. The culture is . . .

Writing fiction has an advantage in that short stories do get published and many more novels get published each year than plays and screenplays get produced. It is possible to make a living writing fiction. It also gives the experienced writer more control over the final version of his work. Successful books can provide additional royalties for a long time if you or your agent monitors success. I daily shave a man who receives small royalty checks twice a year for work done half a century ago.

Class: See Social Class

Clichés

Metaphors, similes, and expressions that are familiar and tired from overuse should be avoided wherever possible in fiction and nonfiction. In an ideal world, clichés would be limited in conversation also, but we get hooked on cliché expressions early in life and they become part of our spoken language. Don't fret about the natural tendency to fall back on clichés as you write a first draft. Second and later drafts will enable you to think about fresh ways to accomplish the same thing. Clichés are familiar, as in "Will you please sit down." "Please sit" works just as well. Adding a touch of sarcasm, as in "Will you sit down now or later?" if warranted gives us a touch of conflict. See **Adjectives and Adverbs**.

Collaboration

I have seldom edited collaborations except out of necessity. I did supervise and edit a nonfiction collaboration on a hot topic that had to be published quickly. While the book had a good life on the bestseller lists and has become part of its time in history, it was difficult to meld the two writers' convictions and to some degree their styles. Most book-length collaborations are of nonfiction unsupervised by a third party, the official editor, until the manuscript is complete. In the writing of novels, collaboration can be exhausting and counterproductive because a novel is one person's intense vision of characters, their thoughts, and their adventures. No two people—not even biological twins—have enough in sync to be able to, say, write alternate chapters of a novel. In the time it can take to write a novel, the writer is sometimes tempted to show his work in progress to a layman. Laymen can point to what they see as flaws, but at least as often the advice of amateur editors can wreak havoc with a novelist's work. Beware especially of suggestions to *tell* what is happening when it should be *shown*.

Commas

This punctuation mark used to separate items or clauses in sentences can also be a provider of rhythm in writing. For instance, commas can set off clauses that increase in power or meaning in the course of a sentence. "He dressed nattily, nearly always wore a hat jauntily, had an answer for every current subject, but Ellen found him a bore."

Commercial Versus Literary

In fiction and nonfiction alike, this dichotomy is not always instructive. "Commercial" includes such genres as the crime novel, the suspense novel, the romance novel, and at worst a potboiler written solely for the money. In nonfiction certain popular books of instruction appeal to large audiences who want to learn something, often the output of popular psychology. Some novels written in a commercial genre are quite well written, but in them human nature is predictable and often superficial or conventional. Some commercial novels have been written by well-educated and resourceful people who like to write what they like to read. Commercial novels are often written in series with the same protagonist. But so are the Sherlock Holmes stories, in which the characters rather than the plot predominate. Graham Greene started out with crime novels that are characterized as literary only because of the author's reputation for his later books. Greene moved up quickly to more complex stories with greater emphasis on the workings of human nature. He correctly described his early work as "entertainments."

Literary writing, both fiction and nonfiction, involves the reader in human experience past and present and informs with grace the most fundamental ideas that a meticulous use of language permits. Without literature we are barbarians enjoying solely the entertainment of stories. It is in the literary sphere that we find stories that don't grow old and that come down from previous generations as well as from our own, with ideas that propel themselves into our memory. As a publisher I was surprised from time to time by how well some serious books sold. The publisher has a great responsibility in this matter. The first book that I fought for had been remaindered by its publisher, who had sold about a thousand copies. The edition that I caused to be published was changed in no way except for an introduction about the author, but it was published differently and sold half a million copies in its first revival year. Literature is a publisher's responsibility. We humans have much to learn, and our easiest universal access to that knowledge is in literary writing that lasts.

Conflict

In fiction, conflict is usually between a protagonist and an antagonist, but it can also be between friends, between business associates, and within a family. Conflict is a part of life that interests readers more than peaceful caring. It is usually generated in fiction by a character wanting something or some condition, wanting it badly, and not being able to have it because of the resistance or enmity of someone else. Even the slightest hint of conflict can sometimes be of value. For instance, "As they stepped out, she said, 'It's warm outside.' He said, 'Not warm enough.'" If you're writing fiction, think *friction* from time to time.

An air of conflict can be established through disagreement or contention, and stronger conflict can be the result of quarrels, discord, antagonism, hostility, struggle, fist fighting, combat, and war. Conflict can be between people and their environment, between people and animals, and between groups, gangs, and armies, but such conflict is seldom as moving in fiction as conflict between two individuals. A mistake often made by beginning writers is to think of conflict only in physical terms. Conflict can be within a person, for instance a choice that has to be made between two actions that are likely to have very different outcomes.

Continuing Characters

Novelists sometimes fall in love with one or more characters they have created. A question arises: Do the characters age? Unlike us regular folks, they can age or not in subsequent books. George Thomassy came to life in my 1971 novel *The Magician,* and didn't age through *Other People* and *The Touch of Treason,* though the novels are quite different otherwise. At this moment I'm completing yet another novel and there he is, and even his beloved Francine is still twenty-seven. I love them both as they are. I wouldn't mind staying the same age myself; wouldn't you?

Converting Screenplays and Theatrical Plays into Publishable Fiction

This is a subject not usually touched upon in writing courses or conferences. It was my lot to have experience in this area that proved valuable and I thought I should pass it on. Thousands of new books are published every year but very few new plays are staged professionally and even fewer movies are made from original scripts. I suppose a lot of writers of plays and screenplays shelve the material if it is not sold, but in my younger years I had a reputation for not letting "No" mean "No." Here's the sequence of events that you might consider if a play or screenplay does not get bought.

I'd had a long poem in the form of a dramatic dialogue published in a New Directions hardcover anthology that caused several people to ask why I didn't write a play. I did, a verse play about Napoleon and Josephine, which in retrospect sounds like an act of insanity to me, since only one other playwright in the English-speaking theater, Christopher Fry, was still writing verse drama. However, thanks to Thornton Wilder and the New Dramatists organization, the play was shown to the public at the ANTA Theater in New York with a first-rate cast, won a prize, then was done in California and got good reviews, and I was temporarily hooked.

So I wrote a contemporary play called *Love or Marriage,* which was staged at the Actors Studio, again with first-rate talent, and almost immediately bought by Lord Delfont for production in London. Bear with me. Peter Coe was signed to direct and Michael Rennie to star in the male lead. Soon enough Delfont, Coe, and Rennie were at such odds that none of them dared pass an open window when the others were present. Out of anger that nothing was moving forward in London I sat down at my typewriter (yes, my dear young friends, a typewriter) and in seventeen nonstop angry days turned the play into a novel and sent out six copies to paperback publishing companies as written by Anonymous. My day job was in publishing at the time. And five of the six recipients assumed I was looking for a reprint deal. Five were interested. One of the five guessed who wrote the book. To cut this short, the book was taken by a hardcover publisher, Coward-McCann, under a new title, *The Husband,* followed by six printings of the paperback, with each cover sexier than the last. Books were a lot more hospitable than theater, so I wrote a novel not intended for the stage, *The Magician*, which luckily sold more than a million copies, was taken by the Book of the Month Club, and—get this—was bought by 20th Century Fox for a movie that was never made. In 2009 I saw a play in New York that reminded me in general terms of my own *Love or Marriage* and the novel *The Husband*, which I later updated as a contemporary play. What goes around, the cliché says, comes around. The point being that plays and screenplays can be turned into novels and vice versa if you have an interest and some knowledge of the different fields, some of which is supplied in the book that's in your hands right now. I have minimized the emotions I felt during the above events, but those emotions when recalled have infiltrated at least nine novels I have written since.

Craft Techniques

These have been developed mainly by fiction writers over many years to facilitate the reader's imagination and his belief that what he is witnessing is true. In other words, craft techniques are used to get the writing free of the writer so that the writing can stand independently and, if good enough, last even longer than the writer. Narrative nonfiction uses some of these techniques to establish interest, credibility, and durability for the narrative. Nonfiction that conveys information or instructs has a few similarities; to make facts interesting they can be presented in a human context, if appropriate.

Creating Emotion in Fiction and Nonfiction

As a reader, when you're moving through a finely crafted story or novel, your emotions are on edge and you want the real world not to interrupt your journey. The big mistake made by some writers is forgetting that it is not how they feel but how they make the reader feel that counts.

Many of us when young will have a school hangover. We are taught to get the facts down. That's fine for most people but not for writers, who need a different mind-set. In narrative nonfiction and even journalism (if there is time), you will want to spark a reader's emotion when you can do so in reporting facts. In press stories of orphaned or poorly dressed children, if there is no photograph, let the reader see a face or the feet or a relationship to a worried mother. A reader's emotions will make your story more memorable, but be sure to show the evidence rather than tell the reader what the emotion is.

In an accident, a bystander's comments can serve a story. So can a policeman's. You are creating emotions in the reader to supplement the facts in order to make the reading experience more interesting. Conveying information can be strengthened by evoking emotion.

Creating Emotion in Film Writing

A well-crafted screenplay can provide a director with opportunities for involving an audience's emotions. Example: Character A is a woman. She is crossing a street with a lot of traffic as a dancer might, avoiding one car and then another. Character B is a man who sees the woman dancing through the danger until she arrives a bit breathless on the man's side of the street. What happens next is up to you, the writer, but you have established visibly the basis for emotion.

A warning: Hollywood used to trust subtle creations of emotion. Think of seeing Charlie Chaplin waddling away with his umbrella. Good directors still provide subtle emotions, but they are up against producers and studios who want a big bang for their buck. Example: I once saw Elia Kazan directing an important scene in a movie based on a novel of his. The scene involved a car crashing into a truck intentionally as if the driver might be attempting suicide. Kazan, knowing me to be an easterner who didn't like cold, sent someone for an overcoat from the costume department, which he had me put on before he sent me way up to where the cameraman was prepared to film the shot from on high. This is what I learned:

The stuntman driving the sports car and the stuntman driving the truck were buddies, and in a few tries one or the other braked a second or two too soon because he didn't want to hurt his partner in the other vehicle. In the next shot, the talented cameraman zeroed in close to the left front wheel of the car. I saw the close-up of that one wheel bending slowly and found it very moving.

All of a sudden there was a rush of people around the director. I learned later that front office people were demanding a real crash because the scene was costing the studio a quarter of a million dollars. Well, with worried stuntmen on the job, they ended up strapping a sports car that was dropped under the truck at the moment of collision so that no one would get hurt and there would be a big crash that didn't move me—or the movie audience later—as the bending of the one wheel had. This exemplifies the problem Hollywood presents for writers as well as directors. The bosses are not intent on the emotions of the audience. They want a splash of excitement, not a scene in which the hero's near self-destruction is evidenced by the slow bending of one wheel.

Exercise: If you're a novelist writing a screenplay, watch a few great motion pictures to see how small actions, even a line of dialogue or an expression on a face, can generate emotion.

Creating Tension

Psychiatrists try to relieve stress, strain, and tension. Writers are the opposite. They create stress, strain, and tension. Readers hate tension in life but they love it in fiction.

Sudden stress causes the adrenal medulla to release a hormone into the bloodstream that stimulates the heart and increases blood pressure and blood glucose concentration. The result is an adrenaline high that excites the reader. The excitement of tension, which is brief, is not like suspense, which can last for a while, sometimes a long while. Tension is like the stretching out of a rubber band. A novel needs respites from tension. Tension can come back quickly if, say, a character orders another character to do something and the other character refuses. Tip: Creating tension of this sort over something important can be a great way to start a story or a novel. In mysteries and thrillers, tension can result from imminent danger. In literary novels, tension can be the result of a realization that is frightening. When one person knows of a death that the other person doesn't yet know about, the reader will tense up. By mastering the relatively easy creation of similar situations, a writer is able to affect the reader's apprehension, which is one of the pleasures of well-wrought fiction.

Credibility

It goes without saying that nonfiction must be true to what it is portraying for the reader. For fiction, credibility must be established for every action. If a character walks into a room, it's easy. But a sudden meeting of one character with another or several characters with others must seem true rather than contrived, and establishing that truth is one of the more difficult essentials of craft because it requires credible invention. For instance, just moments ago I had occasion to write a scene in which a woman and her fiancé drop in to a busy lawyer's office. The visit is not by appointment. The woman is the lawyer's daughter. She and her fiancé need to consult with her father urgently and to get the father's help in a matter that is critical to the younger people. The father has a client waiting. When his assistant tells the father about the arrival of the two young people, he has to quickly concoct a way of postponing the waiting client without unnecessary upset. Having the client waiting and then changing his appointment for another time fortifies the urgency of the two younger people showing up unannounced.

For every scene in which an action might seem frivolous, or unrealistic, the planting of credible motivation is essential.

Criticism, Handling

If you expose your draft to professionals—agents, editors, or successful writers—you need not instruct them. But writers, particularly beginners, will solicit readings and reactions from friends. The latter can be valuable only to the extent of their pointing to faults you may (or may not) agree with. You're better off asking them to tell you *only the faults they see*. When getting criticism from other writers you respect, or agents and editors, pay careful attention to their comments, pro or con.

I have a method that may be valuable only to me, but it's a useful way of getting comments from laymen. I ask them to put a check mark in the margin next to anything they like especially. For fiction, I also ask them to put a double check mark next to anything that moves them particularly. Given the right reader, this input can be valuable because it will heighten your awareness that your fiction needs to entertain and move your reader and your nonfiction needs to inform. Consider their reaction an interim report card, advising you where you're doing your job best.

Crucible in Fiction and Nonfiction

A crucible is a closed environment from which characters—often antagonists—cannot readily escape from each other. A family can be a crucible. Perhaps the best-known crucible is a lifeboat, in which there may be considerable conflict but no escape. A family in a highly mortgaged home can also be a crucible. Business partners, one good, one bad, are in a crucible. Robinson Crusoe and Friday are in a crucible. In my novel *The Magician* a high school is a crucible because neither the protagonist nor the antagonist can just get up and leave school.

A crucible may also bond individuals who oppose each other in a physical or psychological confinement.

A closed environment can provide a stressful relationship: astronauts aboard a spaceship, vacationers in an island paradise, or crewmen aboard ship as in that great American novel *Moby-Dick*. Playwriting can also benefit from the concept of a limited space becoming a dramatic crucible. Witness Jean-Paul Sartre's brilliant play *No Exit*, in which four characters are confined in a single room and hell becomes other people.

D

Detail

Detail is the salt of prose. This applies as much to nonfiction as to fiction. Most of us rush through busy lives getting general impressions of our surroundings. We are not schooled naturally to notice the differences that distinguish common objects and people. If you train yourself to make specific observations of people and things you can freshen your writing with detail. For instance, about two feet away from where I sit there is a huge floor-to-ceiling sliding glass door that lets me see a quite marvelous view of the widest part of the Hudson River. If I were writing about it in fiction I could mention the stunning breadth of the river, but in nonfiction I might say it is 3.6 miles wide at a given point, and let the reader's imagination do the rest. Facing me beyond my computer screen is a wide bookcase from which books are extracted frequently and not as frequently put back neatly, thin books leaning on fat books for their support. You can characterize nature, the artifacts of mankind, and people by noticing and using detail. We can train ourselves by starting with something simple. Many people will glance at a watch on their wrist several times a day, but have any of the people in your narrative ever glanced at a watch? Glancing at a watch can be cautious or rude, either of which characterizes. Clothing is useful for detail, but beware both the cliché and the unlikely. What would a well-dressed man with a shoelace trailing feel or do if he was in the middle of a crowd in Times Square? Or at a wedding service where one could not rescue the shoelace because the pews are too close together? A writer notices and invents the minor difficulties of life as well as the big ones on which plots are based. But the same writer needs to note a grandmother who is smiling broadly for the first time in years because . . . (over to your imagination).

Developing Drama

The essential method used at the Actors Studio: Each person in a confrontation has a different script in his or her head. In private the director tells Character 1 something about the other person in the oncoming scene. Then in private he tells Character 2 a different and conflicting story. The minute the scene starts, the emotions created are high because the facing actors have different scripts or views. The complete description of that process is in chapter 7 of *Stein on Writing*. This principle works in fiction as well as in plays and screenplays:

giving opposing characters different and opposing information about the same matter.

Dialogue

Think of dialogue as a powerful language. It can make people laugh, cry, and believe lies in seconds. A few words of dialogue can carry great meaning. In the theater it can result in thunderous applause from people who have paid heavily for the privilege of listening to your words. Too few writers, however, fully realize how few words are needed for dialogue to be effective.

> SHE: *Hello there! How are you?*
> HE: *On my way to jail.*
> SHE: *Good God, what are you planning to do?*
> HE: *It's done.*

Note that this exchange raises more questions than it answers, which in dialogue intensifies the reader's interest. Dialogue can also reveal character quickly:

> SHE: *I see you're feeling better.*
> HE: *Since when can you see what I feel?*
> SHE: *I thought this was going to be a peaceful discussion.*
> HE: *That was yesterday.*

In any dialogue, if you find yourself strongly on the side of a character, consider making the opposing character stronger and even letting him win the argument.

In my book *How to Grow a Novel* I have a succinct list

of ten points worth considering when writing dialogue. They are:

> 1. What counts in dialogue is not what is said but what is meant.
>
> 2. Whenever possible, dialogue should be adversarial. Think of dialogue as confrontations or interrogations. Remember, combat can be subtle.
>
> 3. The best dialogue contains responses that are indirect, oblique.
>
> 4. Dialogue is illogical. Non sequiturs are fine. So are incomplete sentences, and occasional faulty grammar suited to the character.
>
> 5. Dialogue, compared to actual speech, is terse. If a speech runs over three sentences, you may be speechifying. In accusatory confrontations, however, longer speeches can increase tension if the accusations build.
>
> 6. Tension can be increased by the use of misunderstandings and impatience, and especially by giving the characters in a scene different scripts.
>
> 7. Characters reveal themselves best in dialogue when they lose their cool and start blurting things out.
>
> 8. Think of the analogies with baseball and Ping-Pong as a way of understanding how dialogue differs from ordinary exchanges. In life, adversarial or heated exchanges tend to be repetitive; in dialogue, such exchanges build. In life, adversarial exchanges vent the speakers' emotions; in dialogue, such exchanges are designed to move a story forward.
>
> 9. Avoid dialect if possible. It makes readers see words on the page and interrupts their experience.

10. In dialogue every word counts. Be ruthless in eliminating excess. All talk is first draft. Dialogue is not talk. At its best it is confrontational, personal, and charged with energy.

Dialogue, Advanced

One of the errors one encounters in dialogue by an inexperienced writer is the directness with which A tells B something that is emotionally moving and is important to the story. Such dialogue conveys facts, especially with bad news. What the writer should be striving for is to evoke the emotion of the bad news *in the reader*. Here's an example picked at random from a novel in which a young woman named Susan gets a middle-of-the-night call that wakes her. She knows it comes from abroad because the operator says, "*Un momento,*" and she immediately hears her mother's voice saying, "Susan, it's me."

"Where are you?"

Why do we first assume that a call from overseas is a call from nearby? Is it because we still cannot credit the clarity of sound bouncing off a satellite and coming down to earth in the exact spot next to your ear that the caller was aiming for?

> "What is it?" I said, wide awake.
> Her next words were like dry biscuits breaking.
> I said, "I can't hear you."
> "I have to . . . to talk to you, Susan."
> "You *are talking to me, Mom.*"
> "I don't know how to tell you."
> "Tell me what?"
> "Love, Dad's been killed."
> "Mom, would you say that again."
> "Oh Susan, I don't want to."

"Did you say he's been killed?"
"Yes."
"Did you say yes?"
"Yes."

All of this could have been done in two lines but it wouldn't have generated the emotion that the reader will feel. Efficiency is not the goal. Creating emotion in the reader is. A character might be sitting down on a leather couch, noting the smell of the leather, or looking up toward a restless sky at weather that might help a trip with bright sunshine or suddenly cloud over and change everyone's expectation and mood. A good exercise is to examine your own work for places where you've taken shortcuts, made a quick communication to the reader, and should change it to create an experience, however small or large.

You can also use this kind of extension of dialogue to convey relationships. Here's a small scene many years earlier of the same Susan and mother in the example above.

> Once, when Susan was just four, I took her with me to the central library's large reading room.
> "What are all these people doing?" she asked me in full voice.
> Several people turned around to shush the little girl.
> "They're reading," I whispered.
> She wiggled her finger for me to bend over toward her. "Are all of them reading everything?" she whispered.
> I shook my head.
> Loud enough for everyone to hear, Susan said, "I am going to read everything!"
> Outside, I squeezed her hand in approval. Susan squeezed my hand right back to show she approved of my approval.

The reader sees the scene of the little girl and her mother in the library. If that were all, the bit wouldn't be worth doing. The way this author handled it, the reader is right there in the library witnessing the exchange and incidentally learning that Susan is likely to grow up with a hunger for books.

Elmore Leonard's novels have characters that are characterized by the omission of words. For instance, "The fuck you drinking?" Left out are "What" and "are."

In my novel *The Best Revenge* an elderly and powerful Italian omits words as in the following: "Clara go two colleges, last one where all snob girls go, whats is name?"

The first clause has an omission, the second a crushing together of "what is its name?" The character also uses a phrase common to non-English-speaking people: "I tell you something."

Diction

In writing, diction relates to the choice of words and phrasing. In nonfiction, precision and clarity are the goals to aim for. In fiction, the writer's capacity to choose words carefully for their effect as well as their accuracy is a measure of the writer's literary ability. The opposite of careful diction is "top-of-the-head" writing, words put down as fast as they come to mind, without revision for accuracy and effect. It is found most often in hurried popular writing in which communication of content or story dominates the precise and fresh use of words and expressions. See **Grammar Switch** for "freshness" in writing.

Drafts

How can you tell the amateur instinct from the professional instinct? The answer is in the writer's attitude toward drafts. The economist John Kenneth Galbraith, with whom I once shared a meal and a platform, was one of those rare authors whose table talk was both knowledgeable and entertaining. He is credited with saying, "I do not put that note of spontaneity that my critics like into anything but the fifth draft."

A writer is a craftsman who is prepared to write new and better drafts to perfect his work. The nicest compliment one can receive from another writer is when he or she asks to see more of your work. I sent Saul Bellow, a tennis adversary in my youth, half of the eleventh draft of my novel *The Best Revenge*. That half ended with a scene in Chicago, long associated with Bellow, though he was born in Canada. The reply I had from him was "You can't leave me in Chicago!" I sent him the second half of draft eleven and then my publisher pounced for a quote. In the meantime I had written two more drafts, and I must say there is a lot of gratification in being able to improve writing that is satisfactory. A professional editor may run away from a writer who says, "Do I really have to do another draft?" If one can imagine a heaven for writers, one can see a long line of famous dead writers standing in line and hoping they will somehow get a chance to do just a little polishing of their masterpiece.

Drama

The director Elia Kazan used to say that drama consisted of two dogs fighting over a bone. That's a strong image, useful as a reminder. A tamer version has drama consisting of two strong individuals, each highly motivated, with strong desires and at least one admirable quality, clashing.

E

Eccentricity

This is much more important in fiction than most beginning writers realize. In novel writing we are trying to create individuals, people who are not robots out of the same factory but quite different from each other. The better the writer, the more individual the leading characters seem. This understanding is sometimes absent because we often think of eccentric people as social nuisances. Characters in fiction need to seem at least somewhat special or different. Ahab is not your everyday ship captain. Nor is the whale just a whale.

Editing and Editors

Editing is a noble occupation for which no Nobel Prize will ever be awarded. The editor's job is not to redo or rewrite anything in a story, article, or book, but to see that a manuscript can reach as close to perfection as is possible given time, will, circumstance, and an author who understands and appreciates the relationship. As a novelist I've experienced the range of editors, from one who just marked up the manuscript and expected me to agree to everything he did (and learned otherwise), to the late, great Tony Godwin, who challenged my writing and kicked me up to an entirely different level. Great editors are, as it were, silent partners to the writer. Some editors become not only confessors and collaborators but also confessors and friends. In the words of Jonathan Galassi, chairman of Farrar, Straus and Giroux, the editor "must be politician, diplomat, mediator. He is a double agent" who represents the publisher who employs him and the writer to whose work he is committed. Editors train themselves to be calm in difficult circumstances, but let themselves be warm and enthusiastic when the news is good. They deserve much more than the thank-you in the acknowledgments for their backstage contributions.

The important relationship between a writer and his editor is rarely shaken, but I am aware of an instance in which a high-ranking editor on his own turned eleven sections of a novel entirely into italics, which made no sense and alarmed the author when he saw the proofs. The author in this case had published many books and knew the president of the company well. One phone call and the unwanted italics vanished. The editor who didn't consult the author about a major weird idea soon went to another company. The book nevertheless received outstanding reviews.

Editing, Need for
I've met writers who believe that their manuscripts need a little this and that, which confuses editing with copyediting. The latter involves straightening out the author's grammar, repetitions, facts that need checking, and suchlike.

Copyediting is a highly skilled and usually underpaid craft. We're talking about getting a story right, which requires an editor with knowledge of how successful works have been written, of the extensive and subtle crafts of fiction or nonfiction. An editor will suggest word and phrase changes and make helpful suggestions for improvement of a work in order for it to be reviewed and published successfully. The editor has to appraise the author's execution of his intentions and to suggest ways to improve, if needed, characterization, plotting, dialogue, intelligence, and freshness.

To understand thoroughly the editor's role in the perfecting of worthy works, I suggest a careful reading of volume 1 of *The Paris Review Interviews,* which will deepen your view of the editorial job as witnessed by Ernest Hemingway, Joan Didion, and Dave Eggers. In my memoir I devote a chapter to an experience from the editor's side of the table, a first novel that came to me after it had been rejected by another publisher. I read the rejected work and spent three months working, arguing, suggesting to the author, working in person to advise the author in perfecting the book. Was it worth doing? Well, the edited novel made the *New York Times* bestseller list and was number 1 for thirty-seven consecutive weeks, a record. Its title was *The Arrangement* and its author was Elia Kazan, the director of Tennessee Williams's *A Streetcar Named Desire* and Arthur Miller's *Death of a Salesman*. In his autobiography he calls me not his editor but his director and producer. What a director does for actors onstage and on the movie set is in some sense what a dedicated editor does for writers to help improve the reader's experience of their work.

Editing Nonfiction

The nonfiction editor's work is somewhat different from that of a fiction editor. Clarity is a major issue, especially if the pleasure of reading is to be preserved. The road to understanding can have rocks and trip wires. The order of facts is important both for understanding and for ease of reading. The editor must be aware of other books—especially recent ones—in the immediate field to avoid a review that says, "Fine, almost as good as so-and-so's title!"

The editor of nonfiction must be aware of legal issues, particularly in the fields of food and medicine, and most particularly in biography and memoir. The editor may need to consult an outside expert if points are obscure and the author cannot elucidate. An especially touchy area is clarification. The editor is always alert to the possibility of improvements, but a change of words may affect accuracy. If the author is a specialist in a field he may have used jargon that would be inappropriate for the interested lay reader. In most instances clarity can be achieved and jargon eliminated, though authors who have used jargon unwittingly for a long time may require some quiet diplomacy to cure a bad habit. The responsibility of a fiction editor is to point out ways of improving the reader's experience of the story. The nonfiction editor also has to keep the reader's experience in mind when a writer used to writing only for colleagues aspires to write for a larger audience.

Editing, Self-

That's a common misnomer. If you are working to improve your own drafts, you are *revising*, not editing.

Emotion

Fiction and narrative nonfiction are intended to create emotion in the reader. The trapdoor writers can fall through is *telling* the reader how the characters feel. Thus the admonition "Show, don't tell." To say someone keeps tapping a finger is showing nervousness, which is better than telling the reader that the character is nervous. Showing is almost always desirable, but telling is what we often do in life and is therefore a frequent interloper in a writer's work and needs correction at revision time. See **Showing and Telling** and **Dialogue, Advanced.**

Ending Chapters

A long time ago I quoted a then new writer named Joe Viterelli, who ended a chapter by having a character say, "You have two choices, I can kill you or something else can happen. Why don't you wait and see." The thrust of any chapter ending in fiction is to induce the reader to move on to the next chapter. Viterelli did it in the simplest way. There is no reason why in nonfiction a chapter shouldn't end with a tease. In fiction it is even more desirable. In my novel *The Resort* the last four words of chapter 1 were designed to make it impossible not to continue.

In most literary fiction the thrust may be more subtle.

English (the Language)

The lingua franca of the world is not French but English. Bede, an English monk, wrote the first history of English-speaking people not in English but in Latin. Nevertheless, it was Bede who proposed that English should be used in books. Today, English is the required language of airline pilots the world over and is a second language for better-educated people in many countries.

The highest-ranking person to use English in creative work was Queen Elizabeth I of England, who wrote poems, as, for example:

> *I grieve and dare not show my Discontent;*
> *I love and yet am forc'd to seem to hate;*
> *I do, yet dare not say I ever meant;*
> *I seem stark mute but inwardly do prate.*

"Prate" means idle chatter, which this poem is not.

Elizabeth was quite educated, spoke six languages, and translated texts from French and Latin. She was not a great poet but the very fact that she wrote anything in that form makes us wonder, would an American president or a British prime minister be able to do better?

Essays

In school you dutifully wrote compositions according to a formula presented by the teacher. An essay written by an adult is much more demanding. One hopes it to be a composition written with style and flair, not just of interest in the unveiling of subject matter but also written with grace and wit by a thoughtful writer. An essay is something valued as much or more for the rhythm of the words, the examples defined, the pleasure of the writing. An essay can be an exploration, an elaboration, its dominant characteristics the insights of the author and his use of language.

Literary essays that have brought joy to readers over the ages are sometimes tarred with the experiences readers have had with dissertations, theses, treatises, monographs, and similar writings whose intent is to inform and whose form is often without life. There is no sensible reason in the world why a factual discourse has to be dull. This practice is as bad for the quality and joy of written matter as e-mail, which has thoroughly defeated the once artful practice of handwritten letters composed with care. Even a telephone call has a voice, but few e-mails have style or character.

My recommendation to a young writer is to spend some pleasurable time with a collection of essays by various hands. Such reading might improve both thought and style in writing fiction or nonfiction that one expects to have a welcoming readership.

Exercise in Style
When Joan Didion was about fifteen, she took to typing out Hemingway's sentences over and over again. Her style is markedly her own but typing Hemingway sentences helped her develop her quite original style. Try it. It doesn't have to be Hemingway. Pick a writer whose style you like and type away. Yours will be different.

Expanding Fiction from Within
This is a valuable technique too seldom used. When you are writing a longer work of fiction, the impulse is to keep going

with the story by adding to what you have already written. It may sometimes be more effective to expand from within, that is, scenes you've already written can be expanded by things you didn't think of in the original writing. Often these may be the depths of your work, such as what characters think instead of just what they say, or where in the character's biography or history present thoughts come from. For instance, a man and a woman have been dating others sequentially until they meet each other and soon learn that the new relationship is something more profound than they have previously experienced. They explore the differences in dialogue or thought, creating a definition of lasting love in the story.

Explication

To explicate means to make clear. In academic usage, explication of texts is a kind of sport to find hidden or abstruse meanings in literary texts. This is more useful to specialists than to writers and readers. Explication of texts is the specialist's sometimes private wing of literary criticism, suggesting what the writer was getting at or meant. Of course, in nonfiction precision and clarity are of paramount importance, and excavating meanings in fiction often intrudes on the experience of the fictive story.

Exposition

Fiction writers beware! This contamination of the fictive experience derives from early schooling in writing compositions. Exposition provides factual information. The fiction writer is trying to create an experience for the reader, which means that information is conveyed by the words of characters (dialogue) or by description that carries an emotional component, such as "The wooden deck of Henry's lakeside house, bought two generations ago by Henry's grandfather, accompanied one's footsteps with creaky sounds of wood hurting from the trespass of humans."

An Eye for Detail
It's like focusing a camera, a habit of observation worth cultivating. Don't see a man entering the room, see the fact that he's very tall and has to stoop a bit as he comes in. It's the stoop that's interesting. Or see a woman who turns sideways so people can see how thin she is. Singular characteristics are memorable. They should reflect on a character or the story. I've pointed out elsewhere that the film director Henri-Georges Clouzot created tension in a scene of interrogation by focusing on a foot tapping and a hand pulling on an earlobe creating a tension greater than mere questioning. Bone up on the practice by looking around the room you're now in until you notice something you've never noticed before.

I have often wondered if an eye for detail is not the primary talent of successful writers. They see the tail of the man's tie lower than the front. They notice that only one shoe looks polished. That when the young woman shook hands, hers was soft and she was anxious to disengage quickly. Journalists and nonfiction writers can benefit greatly by observing and using detail, preferably something fresh that lifts the prose around it. See **Particularity**.

F

False Notes
Even if you're not trained in music, as a member of an audience you would probably detect a false note in a live performance. Similarly, one can have false notes in writing. An educated woman is more likely to say, "My husband is incorrigible" than "My guy screws up whatever he does."

Family
Newcomers to fiction writing sometimes conjure up an important character that seems to have no relatives or domestic life. In order for characters to seem alive to the reader, it helps to remember that even hoboes have mothers and fathers.

Fast Writing
Ray Bradbury said writers should learn from lizards. The faster you write, the more honest you will be, because the internal censorship machine is a full-time pest you have to outrun. If you can't do fast writing, make sure that your censor is stowed in a closet.

Fathers (in Fiction and Nonfiction)
In fiction, if characters are to be lifelike, it's useful to remember that in life people are not produced by spontaneous combustion but by mothers and fathers. Even an absent or deceased father or mother can be useful in establishing characters central to the story. People take into adulthood certain

memories of fine moments or clashes in childhood that influence their current lives. I was lucky in starting to use parents in a significant way in an early novel, *Living Room*. Years later parents became much more influential in the life of my main characters, through memory and backstory. In two of the novels, I use a parent to introduce the story.

As to nonfiction, one wouldn't want to write a biography, say, without investigating the parents of the subject. In other nonfiction, sometimes in journalism, narrative can be enriched by touching on a character's parent, even as a speculative memory.

Faults, Writers'
Mainly because writers use writing for communication long before they begin to write for public view, we are all susceptible to a flaw in thinking that because we have learned to write intelligibly early in life, we can also write for the knowledge and amusement of others without learning the special crafts involved. There are some intermediate steps. In order to compose writing that has consequences favorable to us, we have to consider the result we want to achieve. For instance, when we wish to write a letter of complaint, we have to think of what might sway the recipient to our cause. For such writings, it is not necessary or advisable to entertain the recipient, though wit is often welcome, but it is important to sway the reader to your conviction that a wrong has been done and that he or she might help you remedy it. Producing results requires purposeful thought but does not require the sentences to be graceful, rhythmic, or entertaining, which may be why so

many business letters are crudely stated or boringly long-winded. The problem is often attributed to inadequate schooling at an early age, when the concentration is on other matters, such as grammar, punctuation, and spelling. Many of the entries in this book are designed to help even experienced writers who may want some reminders that writing for readers, fiction or nonfiction, is a craft and an art that is different from early writings designed simply to communicate. Writing for others to experience is a professional discipline that requires as much study as medicine and law, including much reading in the genre in which one hopes to write well.

Feedback

In all but the work of reporters chasing news there is a window of opportunity for the writer to get an opinion on a draft of his work. Be warned, however, that it takes time and effort to develop a relationship with a feedback supplier, because you will have to trust the views of another who may not have a perspective or taste similar to yours. This is one of the difficulties in writers' groups because members of a class or seminar get opinions that they may not be able to evaluate as helpful or unhelpful, right or wrong, or partly right. Usually there is a leader of such a group, or a teacher, whose status and experience lend gentle authority to his or her remarks, right or wrong. In my college days, if I may be permitted a recollection, I had a writing teacher of some notoriety, who would allow each student one private session each semester. When my turn came, he said, "Stein, your shirt is blue, your jacket (worn in those days!) is blue, your pants are blue, and that's what's wrong with your writing, it's all the same color." It was useful feedback. That same teacher would have us read a certain short story by James Joyce every week during the semester. As the story became more familiar, we read less with an eye to the story and more to how each effect was accomplished. Reading and rereading the work of others, whether or not you like the work entirely, partly, or not at all, provides a kind of craft feedback about your own work.

Here's one piece of feedback you can rely on: In fiction or nonfiction, you can't write the kind of book you don't like to read.

Fiction, First Three Pages of
Readers who have read *Stein on Writing* some time ago may have forgotten about the informal study of book browsers in Manhattan bookstores. In the fiction section the most common conduct for browsers was to pick up a book and read the front flap and then go to page 1. They never went past page 3 before either taking the book to the cash register or putting the book down and picking up another. If your book really gets going on page 4 or later, you're out of luck in attracting the browser.

Fiction, Three Elements of
An "immediate scene" is happening before the reader's eyes. If a scene is filmable, it is immediate. "Narrative summary" summarizes what happens offstage. The third element is "description," which can be of an environment, a particular place, a climate of opinion, a setting for the narrative summary, or

the immediate scene to follow. Three or four centuries ago when the novel emerged as a form, the third element, description, was much in use, as was the second element. In the twentieth century our eyes took over. We were exposed to movies and then television, all of which we could see. The scenes were immediate. More recently, jump-cutting, used in film, also became useful to the fiction writer. Jump-cutting is the elimination of the interstices or linear connections between scenes. The character slams the door and shows up at his destination. In context we know that he drove or took a cab or walked, none of which we need to see when reading. See **Immediate Scene.**

First Appearance (of a Character)

A writer will not want to stop the narrative to show a new character coming into view for the first time. It's best to be selective of the character's attributes, picking a simple way of describing the newcomer, as in: "Clarence ducked under the lintel as he came through the door," which shows the reader that Clarence is tall. Appearance can also characterize, as in "Dr. Koch hunched over as if he were ready to listen."

First Drafts of Fiction

There are pros and cons of thinking ahead. You have an idea. If it's a plot idea, think about the character who will be executing the idea. Is she or he a character that you want to take a short journey with in, say, a story, or is the character one you can live with for the length of a novel? Don't worry if you don't see the whole story in your head—it's most unlikely for that to happen. If a character begins to take shape in your mind, do you know what the character wants, wants now, wants badly and can't have? That will get you thinking about the character's story. It's not your story yet; you haven't written it. It's the character's story because something or someone will be in the way of your character, a really tough obstacle, an obstacle that might seem insurmountable. Good, except for writers who can't think that way. They will set their character loose in the world without a formidable obstacle. Well, let's stop a minute and think about your personal obstacle. You don't have an agent? You need an agent. To get an agent you need a story that's in shape for an agent to sell. The publishing world goes through crises and it sometimes seems as if it's next to impossible to sell a novel. Now that's a formidable obstacle to a writer. Is the obstacle you've thought of for your character as big an obstacle? Or bigger? The point is that you don't have a story until you have the obstacle. You can't force someone to publish your book. Your main character deserves an obstacle at least as formidable as the obstacle you face as a writer. Now turn that character loose. Start writing. Pay attention to what Hemingway said. You can discern what the shape of your story should be by getting a reckless first draft down on paper. Be quick about it. It's only a draft. Take your time with the second draft. Eudora Welty used to do the first draft of a short story in one sitting. Cicero is quoted as saying, "Eloquence stems from an uninterrupted movement of the mind."

First Paragraphs in Fiction

First paragraphs are messengers. A second paragraph, if short, can bolster the message to the reader. Can one introduce the main character, the setting, the protagonist's attitude, his feeling about himself and the world immediately around him, and how he feels at the moment, to pull the reader in? Let's look at an example.

> Entering my reception room is like lunging into a corner of bedlam reserved for people insane enough to be actors. There are always two, three, four of them without appointments waiting, some for hours, energized by aspiration, faces puffed with hope, determined to snare me while I streak, albeit fully dressed, the twenty-two feet to the privacy of my office. Or, as a legend of Broadway would have it, I stop because I am tempted to invite one of them, preferably a woman, preferably striking, in for a chat about her ambitions, a subject she is pleased to talk about as I search her face for the glint of talent that given the right words to speak will cause the central nervous system of an entire audience to tremble. Meryl Streep was not the first or last to sit in that straight-backed chair facing my desk exuding talent not yet recognized by the world.
>
> Today, having combed my freeform hair with my fingers before opening the outer door, I stride in to see Charlotte behind the safety of her desk fending off the insistence of a shabbily dressed man who from the back seems old enough to have retired two decades ago.
>
> Charlotte is trying to signal me with her eyes.
> Use a semaphore, I don't understand you!

The reader has gotten the first-person point of view of a Broadway producer. The reader sees the setting, but, more important, gets the producer's attitude toward the people waiting for him. It also has a tinge of need, for a producer needs actors. And today there's a problem his secretary is anxious to get to him.

First Readers

This is not an official title but characterizes a part of writing that is sometimes even more important than your computer. It is the selection of the first person to read a draft, a page, a chapter, an article, whose opinion or word ("Great!" "Awful") you can rely on. Wives and husbands sometimes fall into this category, but sometimes intimates are unsuitable for the task if you want to continue living with them. Also they come loaded with prejudices good and bad about your writing and person because they usually inhabit the same premises as you do. Convenience is not a worthy substitute for competence and reliability. Early in the period when I turned to novel writing, I had as friends and neighbors a couple, the husband of which was a lawyer specializing in estates, fortunately not yet needed, and a wife who was an omnivorous reader of novels. What interested me is that the woman had a sharp and informed critical sense of what was good or not good in the novels she read, and I adopted her for years as my first reader and nicknamed her "Miss Litmus."

Quite often a first reader can be the person who runs your office affairs and happens to have an acute sense of fiction, its illuminations and trespasses. This has a special value in that you can try out a paragraph, a page, a chapter, at the point when you feel you need an opinion about it. I confess that a right hand in the office can be dangerous if he or she has been working for or with you for some time, for the same reason a family member is inappropriate. Also, assistants can have restricted talents. I had one who was terrific on nonfiction, but not fiction. See also **Feedback.** For a different kind of reader see **Agents** in the "Publishing A–Z" section of this book.

First Sentences

In so-called commercial or thriller fiction, a dead body may suffice to pull the reader in. In literary novels I find that characterization and a touch of conflict can entice the reader. Often the point-of-view character starts the story. I have more than once used a secondary character to introduce the main character right at the beginning. Here's an example:

> *Of course a man like George Thomassy puts me on edge. His voice reaches out to you as if it were a command. If he agrees with what you say, he nods as if expressing approval to a child.*

In this brief example, the reader gets attitude, characterization, and a sense of conflict. Much can be done to raise the curtain on the first scene with just a sentence or two.

Flab

Extraneous words weaken writing. In speech we use too many words. We carry that mistake over into writing. For instance, the previous sentence originally had sixteen words and now, after editing, has seven words that convey the meaning. Excessive words are best eliminated during a first revision. We call the excess "flab."

Flashback

There is a difference between flashback and backstory. Veterans of combat are said to have occasional flashbacks, unexpected quick memories of past incidents. In psychology, a flashback is a recurring mental image of a traumatic experience. Backstory, however, is a scene that happened at an earlier time in the story. Flashbacks are not as useful to the writer as backstory because a quick flashback has to be planted and credible. See **Backstory**.

Flat Characters

A flat character is a character as seen in a photograph, what the person looks like from the outside. If you develop a character from what you know of human nature, you are going in the right direction.

Flat Writing

A "flat" in British English is called an "apartment" elsewhere. In music "flat" means below the correct pitch. When it comes to writing, "flat" generally means uninteresting. The purpose of fiction is to provide an experience for the reader; the purpose of nonfiction is to inform and sometimes entertain. "Flat writing" usually means uninteresting writing that does not have highs and lows. One sees words on the page but they don't provide experience, knowledge, or fun.

Fleshing Out

This is a technique for fiction and nonfiction that is insufficiently used. In writing a draft writers are sometimes held in thrall by the finish line—they want to get the scene or tale or chapter done, as if the goal were dessert. Before moving on to your writing today it's a good idea to take a close look at the last few pages you wrote previously to see if you can add a touch of wisdom or color to description or dialogue as if you were an artist touching up a painting, inserting a dab of words that characterizes or moves the story. What I look most for are phrases that on rereading seem ordinary, but if you delete or change or add a few words, you now see how you can enrich a sentence or a paragraph. You can discard something that is getting in the way of a sentence's rhythm. Perhaps the best use of checking is catching carelessness in the previous day's work. It's like getting a daily second chance of giving life to yesterday's work.

Flow

The word makes one think *smooth, orderly*. This can be a dangerous notion for mature as well as inexperienced writers. It is a layman's impulse—not a writer's—to be intent on the smooth flow of a story from beginning to chronological end. A smooth flow might work with a patient audience of friends, but for publishable writing it's a good idea to secure the reader's attention and continue in an order that may be purposely bumpy to keep jarring the reader's curiosity.

In sketching the flow of a story, what counts is not what logically happens next in time, but surprises that stimulate the reader's strong curiosity for more. That's when my favored writing tactic comes into play: *Never take the reader where the reader wants to go.* The flow of a story is not a smooth journey from one event to another in time sequence, because suspense interrupts, jostles, twists, to hold the reader. Flow in writing is not a logical sequence of one thing after another; it is full of turns, surprises, and aperçus that raise new curiosities in the reader's experience. The flow of a nonfiction story can also provide an unexpected event.

Fonts

"What's the best typeface to use for manuscripts?" There are two basic kinds of fonts, those with curlicues and those without, a distinction important for writers who want their manuscripts read with ease. Fonts with curlicues are called "serif" fonts. Those without the curlicues are called "sans serif" fonts. The curlicues link the letters in a word. That's important because *we read words rather than individual letters*. Sans serif typefaces are okay in short material like advertising headlines and photo captions. Sans serif faces are sometimes used by designers because they can get more words on the page if needed, but they are cutting down on readability. Now that almost all writers use computers and can choose their typeface, serif types like Times New Roman have become a standard for manuscripts as well as for business writing.

Foreign Words

It's a sensible idea to avoid foreign words that are not familiar to many of the people for whom you are writing. I am frequently surprised and pleased to come across words of foreign origin that have crept into general understanding to the point where they appear in dictionaries. The overuse of foreign terms can make writing seem pretentious.

Format for Manuscripts

Use standard size paper only, 8 ½ × 11 inches. Bright white is easier to read. *Do not decorate any part of it.* I've seen good writing sent back because decoration screams, "Amateur!" Word count belongs in the upper right corner of the title page. Round it off (75,000 words, not 74,289 words). I put the title in boldface and my name under it "by Sol Stein." In the lower left corner is where you put your contact information: e-mail address, street address, phone, fax if you have one; when you get an agent, the agent's name and contact information will replace yours.

Formula (Stein's)

$1+1=½$. Every writer should read at least the first page of Elia Kazan's magnificent autobiography, called simply *A Life*. There is much to learn in the book about theater, film, and fiction. One of his smaller offerings is my formula, simpler even than Einstein's, $1+1=½$. It's designed to show that conveying the same matter more than once in different words diminishes the effect of what is said. This kind of doubling up is a carryover from speech, where we often try to strengthen what we're saying by saying it again in a different way. The fact is that if in writing the same matter is said in two different ways, either way alone has a stronger effect on the reader. $1+1=½$. Copy that formula onto something you can keep in view whenever you are revising.

Formulaic Fiction

I'm not *opposed* to formulaic fiction; I just can't read it for pleasure. It's sometimes called "popular fiction," a misnomer because literary fiction can also be surprisingly popular. The genre called "commercial fiction" is also a misnomer because literary fiction can be monetarily rewarding. I have never read a romance novel, though as a publisher I was responsible for about a hundred books a year. I once edited seven books by a commercial novelist and was very glad of the monetary results. Clever commercial novelists get their stories down to a formula and make their readers happy. On another occasion I got an editorial client whose first novel had received a humongous advance, and I learned a lesson. What that writer reads with pleasure is commercial fiction, and he's intelligent and realistic enough to know that's what he has to write.

Free Association

This isn't psychoanalysis, it's what some writers do once in a while. It's allowing your mind to meander while you drop your guard. If you need a bit of help, reach for a photo album and look at family pictures as if they were of strangers you're seeing for the first time. What comes to mind with each picture? Which provides a related thought you can use to fashion a character in fiction? Or which can help the reader *see* a person in narrative nonfiction?

At this moment there's a beautiful doe standing less than ten feet from where I'm writing. There's a sliding glass door between us. If I open the sliding door, she'd go running off, frightened. She'd find that her only escape route is up a very steep hillock. She could break a leg. The ASPCA would come and put her out of her misery, but what would happen to the fawn she left somewhere? I don't open the sliding door. Later, I learn that the doe ate off the flower heads in a small garden. That's life. Choices. A fragment I might use somewhere. Life is full of providence for a writer who keeps his eyes open for images.

Fresh Use of Words in Journalism

This very morning I came across an excellent example of the fresh use of a word. "Repotting" means removing a plant from one pot to another. In an interview in *The New York Times* with the former SEC chief Arthur Levitt, the interviewer said, "I can't understand why the S.E.C. culls its leaders from the world of high-stakes investment. What about what economists call the 'capture theory,' whereby regulators become co-opted by the industries they regulated?" Levitt responded, "The European system of gray bureaucrats running government agencies forever is far less effective than the refreshing American system of repotting private-sector talent to bring in new ideas." The fresh usage of "repotting" caught my attention and provided a momentary pleasure. Let that set an example. A useful self-discipline is not to turn in a story until you scan your draft to see if there isn't a possibility of at least one fresh use of language. The bonus is that it's habit-forming. You'll also be repotting yourself into a writer who, absent an immediate deadline, uses fresh language when it's possible.

Furniture (in Fiction and Nonfiction)

Some writers are good at creating characters but give short shrift to furniture. Let's think about something as simple as a chair.

We'll call our character Frank. His father had a home within Frank's home, a leather armchair, obviously old, scuffed in places. Frank's mother, Amanda, had her own chair nearby. It was a hard chair with a straight back, which she preferred. She claimed it was good for her posture. Frank was a teenager when he began to understand that his mother's straight-backed chair was characteristic of her entire being, and his father's armchair was so comfortable that after a day's work and a good meal with wine, his father, nestled in the chair with a newspaper in front of his face, would sometimes fall asleep sitting up and have to be gently awakened when it was time for moving upstairs to bed.

As you can see, mother and father have been characterized quickly in a few words about their different chairs. That is one way furniture can be used. Of course, if young Frank was away for a few days and returned one evening to find no armchair he'd be instantly alarmed.

You get the point. Furnishings and many other objects can be used for both characterization and story development if you cause the reader to pay attention to them. I'm particularly pleased to see inanimate familiar objects used in nonfiction and journalism when appropriate.

G

Getting Started

What should you write? You presumably have lived part of your life, and if so, your past is your hunting ground. Gabriel García Márquez, known for his flights of imagination, has testified, "It always amuses me that the biggest praise for my work comes from the imagination. The truth is that there's not a single line in all my work that does not have a basis in reality." Other writers have asserted that they always had to have a character or an incident as a starting point. Since this is a confessional, I suppose that I can declare that from an early age I was an injustice collector; I wanted to right wrongs, which might have made me a lawyer. Instead I created a lawyer named George Thomassy, who appears in several of my novels, righting wrongs for me.

Getting Stuck

It's not a pleasant part of writing, and a writer hopes for a quick cure. Here are some: Get your dictionary, open a page at random, and go down the list of words without reading definitions. Pause when a word interests you. If you're writing a novel, which character might use that word. Which character hates that word because it reminds her or him of what?

If that doesn't work, look up the word "fear." What does your main character fear most? Look up "envy." Which of your characters is envious and why? If you are writing fiction and own five novels, open each at random and read only the top two lines on the left page. One of these tricks will tickle your memory and bring forth an idea that will be useful in continuing your own writing where you left off.

Glitch

Astronauts supposedly originated this word to mean a spike in electrical current. It has come to mean a small problem that can affect a larger enterprise badly. As an editor, I have frequently called glitches to the attention of writers whose manuscripts I was working on. In nonfiction, an erroneous or misunderstood fact is a nasty glitch because it may cause the writer's reliability to be questioned. In fiction, glitches are common in early drafts; a phrase that is not quite right, an inappropriate word for its context, a bland description, a weak sentence, all can be glitches.

I think of a glitch as anything that will interrupt the reader's experience of the story. If there is a published writer who has never had glitches to remedy, I haven't met her. Glitches are the little bugs one gets rid of during revision. I have just read a few pages of manuscript in which the main glitch is in the first sentence. That's like finding a fly in the appetizer served in a fine restaurant.

Grammar Switch

In fiction, a writer interested in freshening his diction might consider switching the ordinary use of a part of speech. For instance, "crowded" is usually an adjective, but the following is an example of a sentence in the first-person mode in which the word is used as a verb, and produces a feeling of freshness: "A crazy thought crowded into my headache."

Guts
A writer writes what other people only think. The best writers have the courage of their beliefs. They give their beliefs to one or more characters and watch them get stronger because they believe. They are not going to keep their mouths shut. Write like you're seven feet high and very muscular; be tough with your characters, your stories, and your readers. They will remember your toughness as a blessing.

H

Hero and Heroine
We don't hear these terms much anymore. The protagonists of short stories or novels used to be called heroes and heroines, but in contemporary fiction the leading characters are sometimes far from heroic. In narrative nonfiction, it is usually helpful to have a central character whose fortunes will matter most to the reader. Today's heroes have flaws and are easier to identify with. They are just as vulnerable as the reader.

High Concept
It's a low term used in the movie business, referring to a brief statement of an idea for the plot of a story that if made into a film will bring a lot of people to the box office.

Historical Fiction

Fiction based on the "real life" of persons who lived in an earlier period has a dual obligation: to be true to the established facts of the period and to be interesting as an experience for contemporary readers. Such fiction competes with published history, requiring the writer both to consider accuracy and to develop a story that will seem fresh to the reader.

Historical Nonfiction, Responsibility of

"The historian has a duty both to himself and to his readers," says Albert Mathiez. "He has to a certain extent the cure of souls. He is accountable for the reputation of the mighty dead whom he conjures up and portrays. If he makes a mistake, if he repeats slanders on those who are blameless or holds up profligates or schemers to admiration, he not only commits an evil; he poisons and misleads the public mind." You have been warned.

Hoarding

Annie Dillard said don't save ideas or images for a later book, use it now, you will fill up like well water with other ideas. I disagree with her. Of course I will use it now if it fits but I won't force it into a current work. I use a small blank-page notebook I bought at the Shakespeare Festival up in Canada, its cover is a blue like none other so I don't confuse this special notebook with others. It contains my future as a writer. I will store a phrase that comes to mind or an idea for a short story or a point of characterization that will make a character come even more alive. I will use the idea now if it fits or store it for later. My guide is not when I get the idea or image; it is appropriateness.

Hooking the Reader

The opening sentences of a story or novel are intended to attract the reader's interest. Literary fiction, short or novel-length, does this gently. Perhaps too gentle for today's readers is E. M. Forster's *Howards End,* published in 1910, which starts with "One may as well begin with Helen's letters to her sister." Today it is Forster's reputation rather than this gentle beginning that urges us to continue.

A subtle hook works fine for literary short stories. Alice Munro, a superb short story writer, began her story "Runaway" with "Carla heard the car coming before it topped the little rise in the road that around here they call a hill." The scene is set visually and a car provides a gentle spur to the reader's imagination: Who is arriving?

Bernard Malamud builds the opening of *Dubin's Lives* with these sentences: "They sometimes met on country roads when there were flowers or snow." It is a fine beginning of a love story. The author continues sentence by sentence: "Greenfeld wandered on various roads. In winter, bundled up against weather, Dubin, a five-foot-eleven grizzled man with thin legs, walked on ice and snow, holding a peeled birch limb. Greenfeld remembered him tramping along exhaling white breaths. Sometimes when one was going longitude and the other latitude they waved to each other across windswept snowy fields."

Malamud provides no commas that might get in the way. His first sentence alone would do for an opening of a love story. But the first paragraph builds sentence by sentence with quiet actions.

Saul Bellow's 1970 novel *Mr. Sammler's Planet* begins "Shortly after dawn, or what would have been dawn in a normal sky, Mr. Artur Sammler with his bushy eye took in the books and papers of his West Side bedroom and suspected strongly that they were the wrong books, the wrong papers."

Bellow was on his way to a Nobel.

The intention of all of the above is to entice the reader's curiosity *gently* compared to, say, thrillers. Originality is sometimes used to entice the reader, as witness John Cheever's opening the reader's imagination in the first sentence of his novel *Bullet Park* with a command to the reader: "Paint me a small rail road station then, ten minutes before dark." The originality is part of the enticement.

Lionel Trilling convinced me a long time ago that fiction is dependent on class differences. I tried such an opening first in a novel called *Other People*.

> When I telephoned Thomassy that morning in March of 1974 and asked him to lunch, I counseled myself to muster a casual voice. As I waited for him to get on the line, I thought the protections are gone. I had reluctantly perceived that civil and well-educated people now accepted gratuitous violence against strangers as ordinary. Therefore I had to conclude that George Thomassy had chosen an appropriate profession in criminal law and I had not.

The title of the chapter is "Archibald Widmer" and Widmer is the speaker. I've used character names as chapter titles in a number of books and find that a simple way of shifting point of view as well as helping to establish whose point of view the reader is now in. But the emphasis here is on class through vocabulary and subject matter.

How Many Writers Are There?

To my knowledge, there are no exact numbers. Agents say that in the United States, there are about a hundred writers who make a living only from novel writing. Agents advise me that most of their fiction clients have day jobs and write in the night and on weekends. Some years ago I was advised that my software programs WritePro™ and FictionMaster™ were being used by more than one hundred thousand writers in thirty-eight countries. That excludes the German-language versions. The number of beginning or intermediate writers, if those terms can be countenanced, has grown considerably from the 1990s into the twenty-first century, given the number of MFA programs and other writing courses and conclaves available in the United States. In my own Fiction Weekends, which were limited to fifty people, I noted that applicants came from at least three other countries and from all parts of the United States; also, one or two writers each time had had books on the bestseller list and were there for a tune-up. One exceptionally successful author actually asked if his agent might attend, too. Nonfiction writers tend to specialize in certain fields and often do most of their writing for magazines, of which there are hundreds, many of them unknown to most writers. The annual *Writer's Market* is available in many libraries and lists the magazines that consider submissions from writers on designated subjects.

How-to Nonfiction

A large number of articles and books are designed to help the reader succeed in a particular activity or use unfamiliar equipment or processes. An example of a bad how-to book is the manual that came with my new automobile. It is nearly five hundred pages in length and has taken many hours to study. Moreover, it came with three additional shorter manuals! Writing instructions or explanations of mechanical detail (and many other subjects) is an abused specialty, possibly because technical writers sometimes work under the thumb of a manager who knows nothing of writing skills. I applaud whenever I buy a new device or gadget and see terse, clear, and brief instructions. Jacques Barzun, professor and later provost of Columbia University, insisted that all writing—even academic writing—be precise and clear. Ignoring this much-neglected advice in academia is relatively harmless because many academic monographs are seldom or never taken out of the library, so their readability doesn't much matter. However, to ignore Barzun's precepts in instructional or technical writing is to steal time needlessly from strangers. If you're heading into the world of instructional writing for the public, revise each paragraph as many times as necessary so that it will be precise and clear. Then check the paragraphs as a whole to see if redundancies worthy of extinction have been left behind. Keep in mind that recipes in cookbooks are also how-to nonfiction and see how short most of them manage to be.

There are many excellent, good, and not-so-good books that instruct how to do something. However, as examples, I refer you to three that are good demonstrations of how well written such a book can be.

Instructional nonfiction depends largely on thinking of the idea. Its content will become a matter of collection. My friend Bill Hutchings had a flash in his brain one day when he was driving his car in unfamiliar territory and wanted to listen to a favorite program of his but didn't know what station number to turn to on the unfamiliar turf. Of course new locations usually mean new numbers on the dial, so Bill invented a book he called *Radio on the Road*. He compiled the information and self-published the book, which went into many printings and was eventually sold to a commercial publisher. At one stage PBS (the Public Broadcasting Service) bought from Hutchings that part of his book that dealt with finding PBS on the road, and created a quick reference manual for its own marketing purposes.

Advice from a Failure by Jo Coudert: Some folks thought that it was a crazy title. Who wanted to learn something from a failure? The fact is that it's about alcoholism and written to a high standard. Fifth Avenue bookshops put stacks of it in their windows. The flaps told what readers would find inside. The book was a huge success.

This Is Your Captain Speaking: A Handbook for Air Travelers was written by Captain Thomas M. Ashwood, national chairman of flight security for the Air Line Pilots Association. It doesn't read like a handbook. It's almost a novel about the experience of flying, what to expect, and it has held up over the years. There's a line on the cover that says, "You'll never be frightened of flying again," and the book delivers. Warning: Since I published Ashwood's book, several pilots have fashioned their own books under that title so look for it under the author's name, Captain Thomas M. Ashwood, if you're interested in instructional writing done well.

I

Ideas

Thoughts usable in a writer's work. John Fowles said that unless he could see his way to three clear days of writing, he couldn't work. Few writers have the luxury of three consecutive days of uninterrupted work, which is why I recommend the following habits to the attention of writers:

1. When a sudden idea relates to a current work, write it down in a notebook because chances are you may not remember it exactly when you get to do the writing. It doesn't even have to be an "idea." Nabakov called it a "throb." Martin Amis called it a "glimmer."

If you're a senior, you must write down your idea, germ, or seed. The question is, where? One summer day I was up in Canada for the Stratford Shakespeare Festival and in the store spied a perfect place to jot an idea down, a slim notebook with lined pages and a pleasing blue cover. It fits into the inside pocket of whatever jacket I'm wearing, which means I am seldom without it. More important, it looks like no other notebook, so just seeing it sometimes gives me an idea. As a publisher and editor I have known many writers, and I am persuaded that the simplest notion can be a starting point for a story if your imagination is intact. I'd bet a half a dozen writers coming upon a balled-up piece of paper on the carpet could come up with half a dozen stories about what's written on that paper. You don't even need that balled-up piece of paper. Anything in your pocket or purse can be the starting point for your imagination.

Observing people in restaurants may be rude to the people you're with, but it's a good source of ideas, almost as good as reading other people's books.

2. Cross out ideas in your notebook that no longer make sense.

3. While writing, if an idea occurs that does not relate to the paragraph you are working on, jot it down in your notebook and continue with your work. The temptation to use an idea right away can impair judgment of the idea and mess up what you are doing. Ideas aren't writing; they are stimulants and need to be particularized before they serve your purpose.

Immediate Scene

In fiction, the action in a scene can be viewed by the reader. If the writer follows the injunction "Show, don't tell" he will have created an immediate scene. One test: If you could film the scene, it is immediate. A stage play consists entirely or mostly of immediate scenes. A nonexperimental motion picture also consists of immediate scenes.

Inspiration

A dictionary will advise you that inspiration is a high level of feeling that makes you want to do something creative, including something mechanical if you're an engineer. Some people credit divine guidance for inspiration. A writer's inspiration often comes from reading someone else's work, observing something in life that reveals an idea, or contemplating an important improvement in one's own work while revising. Inspiration requires an openness to the new, a willingness to be inspired, which calls for learning how to examine and use the small events of life as well as the big ones. A source of inspiration is reading other people's stories and books. I don't recommend copying; I do recommend filtering language and ideas into your own imagination. In time your own previous writing will provide inspiration.

You can also trick inspiration. Open a book you like to any page and copy the first full paragraph. Pick up another book you like and wend your way through a page or two looking for a sentence or paragraph you like. Then put that sentence before or in place of the first sentence of the paragraph you picked. You may be jarred by the concoction but don't be too surprised if the mismatch gives you an idea that inspires you. I learned this from my first two sons, who were only a year apart in age. When the eldest said, "Two and two are four" the younger one quickly said, "Two and two are five," and people laughed.

Interruptions

These can get in the way of anybody's work, but for writers interruptions present a special problem that has solutions. Interruptions may come from something as personal as your bladder, but usually come in the form of some other member of the family, a child perhaps, or the doorbell, or most of all, a telephone. As a writer ages, interruptions increase in danger to the same degree that short-term memory loss sets in. Whatever was interrupted gets lost, sometimes to the serious disadvantage of what you have written. The cure for a writer of any age is to instruct (or train, or beg) others not to interrupt you for anything short of a fire close by. People who phone often during your working hours can be asked to please not call before X o'clock except in emergencies. Friends who use the phone for lengthy chitchat call for two steps: Acquire a phone that lets you know who is calling. While some people understand if you advise them of your working hours, others don't. Don't answer if your phone warns you that an interrupter is calling.

The door leading to my workroom has a sign hanging from the doorknob that says WRITER AT WORK. The doorknob sign works better than a sign on the door itself, which can generate the response "I didn't see it."

During working hours the outer door leading to my living quarters is sometimes visited by delivery people. The friendly UPS man knows to ring the bell and if the door is not immediately answered to leave the parcel at the door. My postman knows I write books (I gave him one) and just leaves oversize mail where I can get at it easily when my work of the moment is over. Even the pharmacist's delivery man knows to hang the bag on the outside doorknob. During a critical period of work, I Scotch-tape a full-size page to the outside door saying PLEASE DO NOT RING BELL. Walter Mosley put it best when he said that we writers traffic in ideas that have no physical form and may disappear at the slightest disturbance. "An alarm clock," he said, "can erase a chapter from the world."

J

Jargon

Expressions used by specialists in many fields that are understood by colleagues in the same field but not by the general public. Writers of general nonfiction intended for the layman should avoid jargon, which obfuscates and hides rather than communicates.

Journal or Jotting

John Cheever kept a frank journal of his life that was very useful to his biographer. I'm of another school. I get an idea, I make a note. Most of these ideas get used somewhere in a novel or nonfiction book. I used to use Post-its, random pads kept in key places around the house, and finally got myself slightly organized by keeping a breast-pocket-size notebook with an easily recognizable cover to closet my random thoughts. Do I use them in my work? More often than not.

One's brain responds to seeing, hearing, reading, and much else, and those fleeting thoughts are part of your collected or recollected new material.

K

Keeping Track of Different Versions
There may be a writer somewhere whose first draft of anything is perfect, but in forty years of editing other people's work in addition to revising my own I haven't come across that writer. And so we will have drafts, each one ideally an improvement of what came earlier. So how can you be sure when you start to work inputting changes that you are correcting the right version? Of course you can title each version this way: Great Novel, v. 1, Great Novel, v. 2, etc. But if you're concentrating on text and have saved more than one version and perhaps forgotten to title the version you now want to amend. . . . ouch!! What I do when I finish my daily work on a draft is check the number of words—computers do this easily—and record the number on a lined card next to the date. This also provides me with a sense of how I'm getting along toward my delivery deadline! At this moment, I am working on my tenth novel, my first memoir, and this book. I have cards for each, with dates and number of words as of the date last worked on. I find this system exact and reassuring.

L

Laziness

This is a BIG problem for some writers unless they are writing on staff somewhere and must submit what they produce periodically to an overseer in order to be paid. Most writers are independent freelancers. As their own bosses, the buck stops with the writers. As a result many writers create work habits, like writing first thing in the day (me) or setting a minimum number of words per day (Hemingway). If getting writing done is important to you, you have to develop a deaf ear to the enemy: other tasks. If you're writing a daily column on a subject that requires little thought, you will in time be able to knock one out in an hour or less, unless you really don't like the idea when it's done, in which case throw it away and start another. But if you're writing a novel or nonfiction of substance, you need to be able to do a reasonable amount each time you sit down to write. If you expect it of yourself, that will help. Also you can invent superstitions, as I have. For instance, when I wrote radio scripts in a tight time frame as a young man (this was for the Voice of America and had to be translated into forty-six languages by 11 A.M.), I learned to start at 5 A.M. in case I needed to modify or scrap the first draft. You might like to invent some rules of your own that you can stick to, but first a serious warning: Most creative writers (fiction and narrative nonfiction) find that they must work every day. Weekends interfere. Holidays interfere. Families interfere most of all. However, one can invent self-punishments to inflict for skipped days. Real sickness is a good excuse. Do not accept imagined or purposeful excuses.

Some writers are helped by setting a minimum word goal for each session. Since you set it, you can break it if you don't have to turn the writing in.

Learning to Write

You also learn to write by reading a lot. Make a list and stick to it. If a book on the list bores you, stop reading, figure out why, and write that down next to the name of the book. Writers are largely self-taught. Especially read the kind of books you hope to write. If you want to write plot-driven stories, that's what you should be reading avidly. If you want to write character-driven literature, that's what you should be reading till your eyes hurt. When you read Kafka, you won't learn to write like Kafka, but you may see how a writer can create unreality that has more of the reality of life than most "realistic" stories and novels. See **Recommended Reading for Writers.** It's far from perfect.

Legal Issues

This applies mainly to nonfiction. To play it safe, express an opinion, which is protected under the First Amendment. If you state the same matter as fact you may not be covered by the First Amendment. Do people and companies sue writers? Yes. Can they cause trouble and expense? Yes. Can someone steal your copyright material? If it's a small amount or part of a review of your book or the subject matter, that's considered "fair use." Keep in mind that nonfiction may be reviewed by the publisher's house counsel or by an outside lawyer. That's for the writer's protection as well as the publisher's. When you're reading proof, be sure the copyright entry is correct. At this writing copyright material is protected for the life of the author plus seventy-five years. This is especially important for books likely to become backlist, because it may eventually provide income to your estate or heirs.

Fiction writers need to be careful about the use of the real names of stores, companies, and people if they don't want trouble. I've seen cases in which writers insisted on using real names until the editor gave up trying for a change—only to regret it later.

"Libel" is defined as a false statement of fact made in print or broadcast about an identifiable living person that tends to bring the person into public ridicule, hatred, or contempt, or to injure the person in his or her occupation or business.

Writers of nonfiction—especially nonfiction relating to food, health, or a public controversy—should take the warranties and indemnities in their contracts seriously.

Collaboration raises legal issues and a written agreement between collaborators is desirable. A sample collaboration agreement can be found in *The Writer's Legal Companion* by Brad Bunnin and Peter Beren.

Line-Editing

There are two kinds of line-editing: the author's own close examination and improvement of a section of a work or of a whole manuscript, and the editor's revising, which comes after the manuscript has been accepted. Right now I am addressing the writer's own line-by-line careful examination of a draft of his work. What are you looking for in this examination?

> **1.** Imprecise use of words.
>
> **2.** Irrelevant or unneeded words, phrases, sentences, paragraphs.
>
> **3.** Missed opportunities. When we talk, frequently used words slide into our conversation. In writing we are aiming for precision. With careful line-editing you will spot places where a more interesting word or phrase might enhance your work. See **Resonance**.

After many decades of line-editing the work of others and my own work, I have come to the conclusion that there is one function of self-editing that can most easily improve any work of fiction or nonfiction, even poetry and plays. It is inspecting *the order* of words and phrases within sentences.

The most frequent change I make in line-editing is a change of the location of phrases or clauses within sentences and paragraphs. This is best understood from examples:

Original: "Helena is the most efficient secretary I've ever had but I had to wave her away despite her stack of incoming mail."

I transposed two clauses: "Helena is the most efficient secretary I've ever had but despite her stack of incoming mail I had to wave her away."

The secretary has interrupted something very important in the story. Readers need to visualize the action in a way that is understood and makes sense as the reader's eyes whisk past the words. The secretary's intrusion with a stack of incoming mail causes the narrating character to wave her away because he is intensely occupied (with his daughter's arrest).

Original: "George, that's crazy!"

I made a seemingly minor change in the location of the name of the person addressed: "That's crazy, George!"

In context, that is a much stronger verbal comeback.

One of the most difficult tasks of line-editing is pace. Pace applies to all kinds of writing. If the words seem to be slowing down, speeding up the pace may help. Successive short sentences can speed up pace. Detailed description can slow down pace unnecessarily. A formula I invented for writing is one plus one equals a half. See **Formula (Stein's).**

Line Space

In a double-spaced manuscript (required by publishers) four blank lines within chapters designate a lapse of time or a shift in location.

Living, Earning a

This subject is surprisingly appropriate in a book for writers who often don't earn a living from their writing during their apprentice years, in which case they have to rely on family members or work a day job and write late at night or very early in the morning. It is a survivable condition given the fact that so many writers have survived that way. A freelance writer (that is, a writer who is self-employed) might find herself or himself on an economic seesaw for a lifetime. If that stops you, you may not be a writer. One good thing about the occupation other than the pleasure of work (most of the time) is that royalty checks may arrive twice a year for a long, long time.

Love Stories or Scenes

The range of love stories is considerable. Love suits storytelling because it is a condition experienced in most lives and can be fraught with incident, conflict, and change. Love can be dangerous because it makes the lover vulnerable. Love scenes vary with the age of the characters involved and their circumstances. Young lovers may be inexperienced, a handicap possibly fraught with fear of being observed, caught, or rejected. External obstacles intrude. Jealousy is a dangerous visitor. Separation can be awful. Elders can be obstacles, as witness Romeo and Juliet. Class differences, incompatibilities, peer pressure, or rivalry from others can complicate stories of love. When the characters are adults, obstacles can be distance, incompatibility in matters other than love, or the intrusion of a competing person.

Happily for the writer, crises may be of many kinds, and love stories over the centuries have proved their attraction for readers. To be credible as well as interesting, the plotting of lovers has to grow out of their characters. The writer can be tempted to *tell* a love story when she should be showing it. The dialogue, actions, and thoughts of the characters should evoke what the characters are feeling.

LOVE SCENE SUGGESTIONS

1. If you're female, write it from the man's point of view. If you're male, write it from the woman's point of view.

2. Plan interruptions that will increase tension and contribute to characterization.

3. Selection of the environment is important.

4. Ideal timing is when the characters are getting to know each other.

5. Figure out what the reader wants to happen at a given point, and then do something different.

6. Use as many of the senses as you can, including intuition.

7. Cliché dialogue is more noticeable in a love scene. Choose your words carefully. Surprise the reader if you can.

8. Remember that you're writing about love, not just sex.

9. Let the reader see what each partner looks like to the other.

10. Remember the forward motion of the scene and its theme, not just the action of the characters.

M

Mannerism

An odd trait, gesture, repetitive physical movement, or habit that may be used as a marker, which see below.

Marker

In writing, think of a marker as a signal conveying a character's state of mind, eccentricity, social class, or other background quickly. Examples of markers: a cap worn backward, answering a doorbell in an undershirt, conspicuously colored or otherwise unusual eyeglasses, badly worn heels on shoes, a man wearing business clothes at the beach, an expression of lifting the eyebrows, an English accent in an American, a person sneezing into the air without a handkerchief, a person tapping a desktop, a person who doesn't normally stammer stammering. Markers are extraordinarily helpful to writers of both fiction and nonfiction. It can be a great continuing asset to be aware of how much markers can accomplish swiftly. Of course a writer should attempt to use fresh markers when possible. I will never forget a character that on first acquaintance had one eye blinking.

Mark Twain's Rules

1. A tale should accomplish something and arrive somewhere. *The Deerslayer* accomplishes nothing and arrives in the air.

2. The episodes should be necessary parts of the story and help to develop it.

3. Characters should be alive, except in the case of corpses, and the reader should be able to tell the corpses from the others.

4. All of the characters, dead or alive, should contribute in some way to the story.

5. Dialogue should sound like human beings would be likely to talk in the given circumstances, and be relevant.

6. The conversation and conduct of a character should be meaningful to the story.

7. The beginning and end of a piece of dialogue should sound like it comes from the same person.

8. Crass inaccuracies and stupidities in dialogue should be avoided.

9. Miracles should be avoided (except in science fiction) and if used should seem plausible, possible, and reasonable.

10. The reader must have a deep interest in the characters, loving the good ones and hating the bad ones.

11. The characters should be so crafted that the reader can tell beforehand what each will do in a given emergency.

12. The author should say what he is proposing to say, not merely come near it.

13. Use the right word everywhere, not its second cousin.

Melodrama Versus Drama

Melodrama is the product of writers who fake emotion instead of evoking emotion in the reader or viewer. The soap operas of early radio and television were frequently histrionic, overemotional, overwrought, sentimental, stagy, and didn't seem to be characteristic of real life. Drama, the opposite of melodrama, features characters who appear to be drawn from life and are engaged in activity that seems both real and moving. Character-driven stories and plot-driven stories can both become melodramatic. Characters in melodrama are often clichés. Commercial fiction and television stories, when skillfully cleaned of melodrama, become more like life. Drama can be subtle; melodrama is rarely subtle.

Émile Zola is credited with killing melodrama. He supposedly said, "I defy the romantics to put on a cloak and dagger drama the medieval clinking of old iron, the secret doors, poisoned wines and all the rest of it would convince no one. Melodrama, that middle class offspring of the romantic drama, is even more dead and no one wants it any more. Its false sentimentality, its complications of stolen children, recovered documents, its brazen improbabilities, have all brought it into such scorn that our attempt to revive it would be greeted with laughter."

Eric Bentley has said, "Zola spoke under provocation of a thousands bad works of art." Here is Zola on what he proposed to do to replace bad melodrama: "I made the one dark room the setting for the play so that nothing should detract from its atmosphere and sense of fate. I chose ordinary, colorless, subsidiary characters to show the banality of everyday life behind the excruciating agonies of my chief protagonists."

"Melodrama," Bentley says, "reduces the spectator's anxiety by relieving him of contact with his own life. . . . melodrama was becoming ever more boring and silly. Stage villains were run off the stage so that 'real life' could return. What Zola is really doing," Bentley says, "is recharging the battery of fear which had been allowed to run down." The substitution of a recognizable milieu for a romantic one plays on the spectator's anxieties because that is where he lives when he is not in the theater. Stage villains were run off the stage so that "real life" could return. Years later George Bernard Shaw conducted a prolonged polemic against melodrama, yet Shaw was still quite capable of producing melodrama himself. Playwrights are tempted by the whoop and fear generated by exaggerations.

"Melodrama," Bentley says, "is human but it is not intelligent." He notes that popular Victorian melodrama exudes the crassest of immature fantasies. Melodramatic theater, he implies, belongs to the magical phase of early childhood, when thoughts seem omnipotent, when the distinction between *I want to* and *I can* is not clear.

Memoir

A book or article covering selected portions of a life written by the person, as distinguished from autobiography, which covers the whole of a life, or biography, which is written by another person. In the twenty-first century, memoir writing has suffered some from tell-alls mainly about dysfunctional families and wayward individuals, sometimes tainted by invention and exaggeration. A publishable memoir, to look at it coldly, should be a literary work that takes the reader into the story of a life and not just a collection of external experiences. It should be well organized, not necessarily in chronological order. Like in fiction, the author has to characterize the people in a memoir, most importantly himself. We should know how the principal people look at various times, possibly how their voices sound, and their other significant characteristics.

One wants a memoir to be and sound like a book of many interesting scenes, not the mere factual recital of a life. In my memoir, I also enjoyed trying to make the chapter titles seductive, as in:

> "Disobeying General Eisenhower"
>
> "When the CIA Was Smart, Successful, and Secret"
>
> "How to Get a Job If the Employer Says No"
>
> "Playing with Fire on Broadway"
>
> "Wedlock: Infants Marrying Infants"

"How to Raise Children at Home in Your Spare Time"

"The Dots That Weren't Connected"

"Assassinating Sol Stein"

etc. etc.

Why lure the reader with chapter titles? Browsers in bookstores usually look at the table of contents in a nonfiction book (a memoir is supposed to be nonfiction!!). And one wants to lure the reader with interesting possibilities. If your prospective reader chooses books online, a tempting table of contents may just lure him to buy or download the book. Originality is worth trying for. The first chapter of my memoir is titled "Hello," and is for the reader and me to get acquainted. My memoir has an interlocutor, a fictional character who is offstage except when he disagrees with something I've said and challenges me (in italics). The interlocutor supplies a touch of conflict here and there. Somebody will outdo this by having an interlocutor be the writer's husband or ex-wife or ex-husband.

Given a decent writing style, I would suggest that the most necessary ingredient is candor, the willingness of the author to see him or herself candidly, not necessarily as a confessional but in the course of beginning to understand the significance of certain events and the necessity of unveiling moments or scenes that shouldn't have happened.

Metaphors and Similes

These are the wonder workers of writing that can lift a plain prose style in the direction of literature. A writer shows by simile the similarity of two things that were previously not connected. Examples:

> "He felt like a million dollars."
>
> "When the doorbell rang she sprang up like a jack-in-the-box."

One has to be careful. Precision in the comparisons is a requisite. A simile that doesn't quite make it can produce a laugh and be counterproductive. A gifted writer can produce a wild simile that works. Consider John Cheever's extravagant simile from his story "The Country Husband": "The living room was spacious and divided like Gaul into three parts."

As for metaphors, my all-time favorite is by Clive James, who said, "Hirohito was a 15-watt bulb."

If you get stuck writing at some point, give yourself a small task. Write a simile about whatever comes to mind or is in front of you. Sharpen it until you make it as good as you possibly can. Then write a metaphor. This exercise will increase your longevity as a writer just as walking distances may lengthen your life.

Minor Characters in Fiction

In one sense there are no minor characters in fiction, because an ineptly drawn minor character can ruin the experience of a scene or its credibility. In *The Magician* a small gang of sixteen-year-olds runs an extortion racket in a high school. We get to know quite a lot about the leader of the gang through his thoughts and actions, but also through his father and through the lawyer who is the leading character in the novel. The goal is to characterize the individuals in the gang when they are together. The other gang members are essentially walk-ons. If they didn't seem credible the plot involving conflict between the more important characters wouldn't work.

In writing for the stage, a walk-on (stage lingo for "minor") character like a maid, butler, or bartender may or may not speak. We know who these characters are by their clothes or place (the bartender is behind a bar). Minor characters must become credible to the reader through passing mentions that have some particularity. "It was easy to find Gary in a crowd of kids, he never took his cap off indoors. Once in a while he'd lift the cap but only to brush his hair back with his hand."

Many writers seem not to realize that a minor character can be unseen and yet occupy a role. For instance, in a work in progress I have a woman in her twenties as a central character, her father as an onstage secondary character of some import to the plot, and a reference to his wife, Priscilla, who is never actually in a scene. At one point in the father's interior monologue we read, "It was Priscilla's idea, not mine, to invite a few of Francine's friends to our party. Fortunately, most of them had other plans." Priscilla does play a minor role elsewhere in the novel, but she is "onstage" merely in thought or recollection. Nevertheless, the reader gets to know that character better through tiny references like the one just mentioned.

Be careful about stereotyping minor characters. Frequent victims of stereotyping are police, waiters, teachers, and parents. Credible minor characters can help make a scene credible, entertaining, or menacing. Their particularity adds depth to a scene.

Monologues in Fiction

In dialogue one character is talking to another. A monologue is a longish speech by a single character, which can be boring. I've used the term "speechifying" for that kind of soliloquy. However, one of the interesting things a writer can do is have a character denouncing another character to the reader, particularly at the outset of a story or book. A speech like that in the right hands can be riveting if credibly done.

Motivation

At an early stage of writing, consider the possible motivation for the important act you expect your protagonist to undertake. Make certain that the motivation is not only likely but characteristic of the protagonist. Challenge the motivation; see if there isn't something worse or deeper behind it.

As for the antagonist, think of the possible motivation of the person in life you loathe most. Even a hurt of long ago can suddenly be of value to you in a story. Sometimes in life wickedness seems unmotivated, but in fiction it had better be motivated or your readers will think you made it up, and that's not what you want your readers to think when they are reading your story. If you're stuck, or in a really foul mood, it's a good time to invent motivation for a character. Fiction is invented storytelling that feels damn real.

Multiple Drafts: A Safety Procedure

During the process of writing, it is commonplace for a writer to have several drafts of a book-length manuscript or different versions of individual chapters. I shave daily a writer who makes additions, changes, and deletions, especially in the case of longer manuscripts. Columbia University is convinced that my drafts and the drafts of writers I've edited are valuable for the education of writers who want to see the changes made from draft to draft. Most writers that I know prefer to bury their mistakes and get rid of earlier drafts. However, even for them, earlier drafts can restore confidence when a current draft is, say, left on a train and never found, as happened with my late friend John Cheever. I have developed a very easy to follow method of identifying drafts written on computer. I keep a lined card on my computer desk for each book or part of a book I'm writing. When I stop, computers make it easy to get the word count. I note the date and the word count on the card. If my assistant is inputting changes I've made by hand, she does the same, date and word count. This system works better then titling drafts as V (for version) 1, V2, V3, which we do anyway, but the exact word count is much more reliable, especially if the writer is of a certain age.

N

Naming Characters
Names should not be treated lightly. The name of an important character can influence the reader's perception of a character just as it does in life. What if Sherlock Holmes had been named Herlock Sholmes? Important: A name that is common can be a liability if many readers are likely to know people with that name or nickname and may be associating characteristics with your character that you don't intend. Try to avoid names of people you know. You may quite unconsciously use some of that person's characteristics instead of shaping the character's traits anew. Variants of familiar names may introduce connotations both wanted and unwanted. Mary is a relatively common name. For an American or British audience, Rosa may connote a foreign-born character. Be careful also to avoid giving different characters similar names, such as Ed and Eddie or Edie.

Some of the most memorable names in fiction mix common first names with uncommon last names, as in George Smiley, Sam Spade, Jane Eyre.

There are class issues in the choice of names. For instance, I used the name Archibald Widmer for the somewhat snooty father of my heroine Francine Widmer. Names should be consistent with the characters' backgrounds.

Don't pick names that are difficult to pronounce unless you want to distract the reader from the story or chase her away. It is important for readers to learn early how an unfamiliar name is pronounced; this is especially true in nonfiction where real names are used. However, some shortening or nickname sometimes becomes the main name of a person, and also can define the status of the person using the nickname. Names can sometimes convey a relationship between the person named and another character. For example, a character with the common name of William might be called Bill or Billy by friends and William by his mother. Watch out for descriptive nicknames like Slim and Bunny because such names can convey unintended connotations. Also try to avoid names that can be either first or last names.

Narration in Fiction
Quite often writers new to fiction writing will tell a story as if they were with, say, a live audience of friends. This form of relating a story in writing comes through as telling rather than showing. Beginners weak in craft are still trying to write stories in a telling mode rather than from the perspective of a character. How do you know that you're "telling"? The use of a narrator telling the story frequently has the rust of yesterday in its air unless the narrator is a highly individual character, in which case you might want that character to be your narrator rather than having a narrator suspended on high seeing your story from a dirigible.

Narrative Hook
Designates catching the reader's attention at the very beginning of a story. Its intention is usually to involve the reader

with a character or a situation in an intriguing way. A famous example is the opening of Dostoyevsky's *Notes from Underground,* which begins: "I am a sick man . . . I am a spiteful man. An unattractive man. I think that my liver hurts. I am not in treatment and never have been." Dostoyevsky is teasing the reader with what on the surface seems to be a nut case.

Narrative Nonfiction

Much confusion has been generated by a change in the techniques of nonfiction writing. One hears of narrative nonfiction, narrative journalism, creative nonfiction, and all seem to involve the emergence of nonfiction from the dryness of mere fact toward what might be called stories that are true, employing some of the techniques developed over time by writers of fiction.

A century ago student journalists were urged to get the who, what, where, when, and why into the first paragraph of a newspaper story. The trouble with that instruction was that readers might invest a few seconds in the first paragraph of a news story and skip to another story. If a journalist had a story to tell that involved characters and color as well as fact, the temptation was to write a feature rather than a news story. Meanwhile, in the world of nonfiction books, the reporting of history by a grand master like Garrett Mattingly seemed to be not just writing about events of long ago, but written as if Mattingly had sailed with the Spanish Armada or had visited Catherine of Aragon and was describing what he had seen moment by moment. It's still nonfiction and true to history.

Narrator

In fiction, the person relating the story. See **Point of View**.

New Dramatists

This organization is dedicated to finding gifted playwrights and providing them with the time, space, and means to develop their craft in readings and workshops. It staged my first play with a volunteer cast of excellent professional actors. The address of New Dramatists is 424 West 44th St., New York, NY 10036. Membership is open to residents of the metropolitan New York City area. National memberships are offered to new playwrights who can spend time in New York in order to take advantage of the programs. Applications are considered between July 15 and September 15. There is no charge to those who are selected.

Newspeak

Moving into the "newspeak" decades, some beginnings have a different voice. Witness Guy Kawasaki's *The Art of the Start*. Kawasaki, founder of a number of computer companies and credited as one of the individuals responsible for the success of the Macintosh computer, is the author of seven books, and writes in the mode of headlines in capital letters, numbered points, boldface points—writing that resembles a PowerPoint slideshow rather than conventional writing. Here's how he grabs his reader's attention at the start of chapter 1:

GIST (Great Ideas for Starting Things)

I use a top-ten list format for all my speeches [this is Kawasaki speaking] and I would like to begin this book with a top-ten list of the most important things an entrepreneur must accomplish. However, there aren't ten—there are only five:

1. *MAKE MEANING.*
2. *MAKE MANTRA.*
3. *GET GOING.*
4. *DEFINE YOUR BUSINESS MODEL.*
5. *WEAVE A MAT (MILESTONES, ASSUMPTIONS, AND TASKS).*

I have omitted the content of the five brief paragraphs because the issue here is the presentation in newspeak, a language that would not and probably could not be read by a nineteenth- or early-twentieth-century reader, who might find the content simplistic and the format objectionable. Kawasaki has a lot of experience and value for business beginners, but is essentially writing—or telegraphing—information in a new mode. His format may hook an audience used to this kind of presentation, but leaves me in love with more conventional English, a language worth loving.

Noise and Interruptions

Serious writing of any kind requires the writer's mind to be in a cocoon of silence where he or she cannot be distracted. Turn off your telephone or cell. I use the kind of earplugs you can get in a drugstore. When someone outside is using a lawn mower or leaf blower, I put on a headset that blocks out all sound including my heavy breathing when I get a sudden idea. Bill Styron said, "No music, no interruptions, a baby howling two blocks away will drive me nuts."

Walter Mosley pointed out that the ideas you get while writing are smoky concepts liable to vanish at the slightest disturbance. On the door leading to my workroom there hangs a small black pillow with a message in white reading "Quiet, please, novel in progress."

Nonfiction as Literature

What a delight nonfiction can be when full of insight and instruction—then it rises to an art. Here is Eric Bentley in the chapter on dialogue in his book *The Life of the Drama:*

> Narcissus used a mirror only because the tape recorder had not yet been invented. Talking is surely, among all the forms of life we know, the prime mode of self-assertion, from the cradle to the pulpit, and from the log cabin to the White House. . . . In their indefatigable efforts to hurt one another, men use a million words to every bullet. For even more than bullets, words enable them to combine the maximum of hostility with the maximum of cowardice.

Notes to Oneself

It will be obvious to the experienced writer that nonrelated fleeting thoughts either while writing or at any other inconvenient time can become inspirations for other writings. The danger comes from such thoughts as *I'll get to that later.* You will but only if you make a decipherable note to yourself the instant you get the idea, because you're likely to forget it, as I do unless I write it down. I keep a small notebook on my night table. It is perfectly possible to get a worthwhile seed of an idea while lolling off to dreamland or on awakening unintentionally at 2 A.M. In fact, writing things down that come at or near the end of sleep has been valuable to me because the subconscious can deliver up some hairy—and useful—memories when I least expect them. If we don't write some reminder words down, it is unlikely that we will ever find these ideas again.

Nothing Happens

When revising, be on the lookout for small scenes in which nothing happens, when there is no real action or change. Consider cutting such scenes to strengthen the work as a whole.

O

Observing

A large percentage of the visual world whooshes by most people. If a writer stops observing details he might as well stop writing. I carry a small lined card folded over in the breast pocket of my shirt so that it doesn't show. Sometimes it's for telling me the address of the restaurant where I'm meeting someone, but often it serves for the recording of an observation of a thing or a person's characteristic. The warehouse of memory is full of fog. Observations in decades past can come to life by stretching out on a couch without something to read but with a writing pad within reach. Close your eyes. Your brain may eventually provide one or two memories that will be useful in what you are writing now.

Opening Scenes in Drama

When writing plays, use dialogue to make the audience laugh robustly even just once. The audience will be in a better mood to accept what happens later.

Order of Phrases and Sentences

In revision, one of the most important and most neglected activities is reading to determine whether phrases within a sentence would be more effective in a different order. I continue to be amazed by how changing the order of phrases in particular can improve both fiction and nonfiction. Try it. You'll be glad you did.

Ordinariness

Beginning writers often settle for characters that seem "ordinary." Certainly an ordinary character can be made interesting by a skilled writer, but I would caution the beginner especially about the difficulty of having an ordinary-seeming character leading a story. Readers are entertained more by an unusual character.

When talking, we tend to use the first words that come to mind. In writing, that tendency most often produces ordinariness. Both fiction and nonfiction deserve better of the writer, which means one should reread a day's work for the ordinary words that might be exchanged for more precise and out-of-the-ordinary words. For instance, a half hour ago I heard someone refer to a political candidate as "an exceptionally strong and experienced leader." It sounds cliché and hollow, perhaps okay for some kinds of conversation but in writing it comes across as ordinary, unspecific, and weak. How different would it sound if on the page it was transformed to "a six-foot give-'em-hell Harry who's been outwitting his opponents for thirty years"? The Harry need not refer to a specific person for the point to sound strong rather than blah.

Orwellian

This adjective connotes an idea or situation that brings to mind George Orwell's novel *1984,* published thirty-five years before that date. In the novel, the protagonist, Winston Smith, who works for the Ministry of Truth, struggles to survive in a totalitarian society in which personal privacy is forbidden and state security governs all. Orwell's novel has been translated into sixty-two languages, proof that his prescience had a universal message. That the message hit its mark is evidenced by the fact that cowardly libraries in many countries banned the book from their shelves.

1984's worldwide success has clouded Orwell's enormous talent as an essayist and journalist. His nonfiction essays and reportage constitute some of the very best writing of the twentieth century yet are too little known and studied by journalists and other nonfiction writers. His style was spare, precise, and clear whether he was writing for news media or posterity. His subjects were, to say the least, unusual. His first-person record of involvement in the Spanish civil war of the 1930s in the classic *Homage to Catalonia* includes the moment when Orwell himself was shot in the throat. An earlier piece, a report entitled "A Hanging," is a close-in witness of the death of a human being and is a remarkable piece of journalism, as are many of his reports, articles, essays, and other nonfiction. In my classes at the University of California, I suggested that students read Orwell's essay "Politics and the English Language" once each year for the rest of their lives. The political subject may not be of consequence any longer but what Orwell wrote about the uses of language is a model of instruction for nonfiction writers today.

Outlining Fiction
Some authors prefer to outline a book scene by scene or chapter by chapter. Too much detail can prove to be a deterrent to the writer's imagination. Much fiction is written without the author's knowledge of where exactly his story is going or how it will be developed in detail. There is a middle ground. A scene outline can be useful if each scene is described briefly, with a suggestion of which characters are in each scene and, say, a note about the main thing that happens in that scene. This kind of brief, skeletal outline can even be a spur to the imagination when the writer is turning it into a chapter.

P

Page Numbering
The location of numbers on manuscript pages seems an inconsequential point, but I distinctly favor the middle of the bottom of the page because down there it does not interfere with the agent's or editor's reading of a manuscript. If the

number is located at the top right of a page, the reader can't help noticing the page number, and it becomes a tiny glitch in the reading process. It's a small matter compared, say, to using an oversize typeface, but I'm all for changing anything that interferes with or intrudes in the reading process.

Paragraph Endings

These are worth studying for their effect. The paragraphs within a novel or a story can and should be different from each other. What to aim for? Whenever possible try to conclude a paragraph in a way that surprises the reader or lures the reader into the next paragraph. It's hard to do when you're writing rapidly, but when you review your work take a good look at the possibilities for surprise.

Particularity

John Gardner told us that "detail is the lifeblood of fiction." I have been reminded from time to time that detail is also the lifeblood of nonfiction. It distinguishes unusual writing from the ordinary. The example I've used is the lawyer Thomassy, who early in *The Touch of Treason* is confronted by the patrician district attorney, Roberts.

> Thomassy could see Roberts's handshake coming at him all the way down the aisle, above it that freckled face proclaiming *I can be friendly to everybody, I was born rich.*
> Roberts's smile, Thomassy thought, is an implant.
> Thomassy moved his gaze from Roberts's confident eyes to Roberts's blond hair, then Roberts's chin, then Roberts's left ear, then Roberts's right ear. *The four points of the cross.* It made witnesses

nervous. They couldn't figure out what you were doing. You weren't doing anything except making them nervous.

Planning a Novel

1. Be sure you know your protagonist well. What does he want? Will that agenda be credible to the reader? Will it seem important? What does your protagonist look like close up? What does he look like at a distance? It's not a bad idea to "live" with a character for a bit, thinking about that character and what his actions and thoughts might be. If you're thinking about your hero, think about his flaws also. If you're thinking about the villain, think about his charm or manners that seduce people into believing he is a nice guy.

2. Choose a theme that is likely to be fresh and to interest people, preferably a lot of people. You don't have to work out details ahead of time if you know what your destination is.

3. What does your character want? Does he want it badly? Does he want it *now*? Why can't he have it now?

4. What is the main obstacle to your protagonist's success? How is that obstacle different from the obstacles heroes and heroines encounter in the novels you've read? If your obstacle is not a person, can you personify the obstacle in a character?

5. What power does the obstacle have?

6. Whatever you've done for your protagonist's character, can you do better with the antagonist's character? The big error at the beginning is to make it obvious that the protagonist will win the conflict.

7. Can you make it clear that the protagonist might lose the conflict?

8. Is the main character you've imagined someone you would like to know better? Why? Don't duck this answer!

9. What is the worst thing a human being can do to another human being? How will what happens in your book measure up to that in intensity or importance?

10. Do you love everybody you know (if so, why are you writing fiction?) or is there someone you know whom you despise but have to see on occasion because he or she is a neighbor, or a relative, someone you'd rather never see again?

Planting

Preparing the ground for something that comes later, often to make the later actions credible. John Fowles, on the first page of his first novel, *The Collector,* begins,

> *When she was home from her boarding school I used to see her almost every day sometimes, because their house was right opposite. . . . She and her younger sister used to go in and out a lot, often with young men, which of course I didn't like.*

Those words and the sentences that follow plant the notion that this protagonist will soon be involved with the young woman in some ominous way.

Plausibility

The quality of making written actions and speech believable. Plausibility is strained or often lost in action sequences that are unrealistic. In fiction that is meant to be historically accurate or realistic, plausibility is a major issue. A character who is drunk may very well speak to a giant rabbit, but travel from one end of Manhattan to another in a minute or two is not plausible. In fantasy or science fiction (e.g., Harry Potter novels), plausibility means consistency within the fantasy.

Playwriting Guidelines

Writing a play is quite a different experience from writing for print. Theater is a collaborative art form. Unlike writers of fiction, who control the universe in which their characters live, playwrights need the talents of other people to be able to see their stories come alive to an audience. Seniority goes to the experienced director much of the time. Actors, particularly experienced stars, will have their say. A set designer contributes mightily to the audience's experience. What the playwright is writing is the frame of a story, creating tension and interest through dialogue, building to peaks of emotion. In the event of success, the time comes when the playwright must turn his words over to actors and a director. One shouldn't attempt playwriting without first seeing many plays (more can be learned from the bad ones). What is done onstage changes over time. See a Brecht play that has direct address to the audience. See Edward Albee's *The Zoo Story* if you can. You can learn to write fiction by reading novels but you learn playwriting by seeing many plays.

Once, in a meeting of a small group of playwrights, Lillian Hellman said, "Anything can be put on a stage." I couldn't help contradicting her by saying, "What about Cossacks on horseback?" Hellman calmly answered, "Anything but Cossacks on horseback." Most plays are about human nature.

If you're writing a play for live audiences to enjoy in a theater, there are a few points to keep in mind. The concentration on dialogue is greater. The optimum length for a play (true also of a film) is two hours if you want to keep your audience's best attention. Of course intermissions, usually about ten to fifteen minutes, are additional. Thus ideally for a three-act play, you would be in the theater for two hours and twenty to thirty minutes. In a long career as a spectator at live theater I've found this information about length to be both true and flexible—but not very flexible. Plays that run quite a bit less than two hours seem short. In my early days of playwriting I had an opportunity to see sixty Broadway productions in two years courtesy of Thornton Wilder's prompting and the arrangements made by the New Dramatists organization, which always provided two tickets, one for a companion, so that a playwright would be seen as a spectator rather than as a student.

The director is the boss during the preproduction period. Afterward, the stage manager keeps the level of the production up. The producer who has supplied the money for the production will determine when the play must close.

Some writers new to theater feel confined by the limits of a stage. They needn't be. Peter Schaffer's *Equus,* a great success in its time onstage, had horses on stage (or stage horses). In a play of mine, I had a woman being interrogated in a raised room while her husband, concerned about her, was pacing at stage level down below. Theater is less confining than one might imagine.

Tip: In revising plays, concentrate on eliminating unnecessary lines rather than adding material. Also ask yourself, What does this play have to say about human nature?

Plot

See **Plotting** and **What Your Book Is About.**

Plotting

A common way of starting a plot is to first create a character (see **Characterization**) who wants something badly and can't obtain it. The need can be as abstract as tranquillity or as concrete as money. But if the character activating the plot seems ordinary or a stereotype, the character's need may not attract the reader or viewer. A serious and urgent need on the protagonist's part, sensed by the reader, is a good way to start a plot. The need should not be immediately satisfied because of an obstacle, frequently embodied in or planted by the antagonist. As the protagonist is reaching toward satisfying his or her need, a new and different need may present itself, fortifying the determination of the reader to stay with the character and the story.

As mentioned earlier, in *Other People* the first character to speak is Archibald Widmer. What he says is designed to pique the reader's interest in him as well as to introduce the main character, Thomassy.

> When I telephoned Thomassy that morning in March of 1974 and asked him to lunch, I counseled myself to muster a casual voice. As I waited for him to get on the line I thought, the protections are gone. I had reluctantly perceived that civil and well-educated people now accepted gratuitous violence against strangers as ordinary. Therefore I had to conclude that George Thomassy had chosen an appropriate profession in criminal law and I had not.

What the Widmer character wants is a lunch date with Thomassy on that very day. Thomassy puts him off. He's busy. Widmer wants to discuss a case in which the victim is his daughter. He finally comes to the point and tells Thomassy that she has been raped, and gets the lunch appointment. The reader senses class as well as occupation differences. Widmer's need is for a lawyer who knows criminal law, and the victim is his adult daughter, someone he cares a great deal about. A brief bit of dialogue ensues and the reader's curiosity is hooked.

Some writers like to start with a location. In *The Magician* the first paragraph characterizes a town in which snow has been coming down for nearly a month. But the key to that paragraph is this ominous sentence: "An occasional older man, impoverished or proud, could be seen daring death with a shovel in hand, clearing steps so that one could get in and out of the house, or using a small snowblower on a driveway in the hope of getting his wife to the supermarket and back before the next snow fell."

That sentence establishes mood, which can also be a subconscious enticement for the reader. Something is ominous about the town. Everything about the town is directed to the reader's need to know what's going to happen in this snowbound town. It is only on the third page that we meet the extraordinary sixteen-year-old magician who is the protagonist. The lesson here is that something as seemingly tenuous as the description of a town can thrust the reader's curiosity forward.

Write what's at stake in your plot. Then ask yourself what would be worse for the protagonist. A lot worse. Then get into a grim mood and write down everything that might make it worse. Put the paper away for at least a full day, then look at whatever worsening you put down and choose the worst that you can handle in your plot. If you're a saint and can't develop bad things that happen to good people, what are you doing writing fiction?

If a writer is a reasonably nice person in life, she will need to draw a curtain around her niceness while plotting, which is devilish work. "He loved her and she loved him and they lived happily forever" is a yawn and neither a plot nor a story. A plot provides specific actions. When writing, a writer is a troublemaker.

Poetry

It is quite remarkable that numerous books of poetry are published every year in the United States. Moreover, a few magazines publish poetry exclusively and some important national magazines feel they must show the flag of poetry at least once or twice an issue. I confess that I wrote poetry when I was young and in one instance a poem I wrote changed my life. A long dialogue poem of mine was anthologized in *New Directions*. People, including Thornton Wilder, urged me to write a play in verse. I was very lucky. That play, *Napoleon,* written in verse at a time that only one other playwright was writing in verse, was produced by the New Dramatists organization in a Broadway theater with a brilliant cast and won the Dramatists Alliance prize in 1953. It was also done in California and received only good reviews. I have a handicap in defining contemporary poetry because I grew up in an age when poems had meter and usually rhymed. Perhaps this inadequacy on my part will prove that I was born in a different age, because I wonder where the rhyme and meter went.

Point of View

This is one of the most difficult craft issues for writers, made unnecessarily complex by some teachers. There are only four points of view and one of them is to be avoided. For simplicity, I will refer to point of view as POV.

First-person POV: I hit him.

Second-person POV: You hit him. The second person POV is intrusive, sometimes polemical, and can disturb the reading experience. The second person usually doesn't work, because it addresses the reader while trying to create an experience in which the writer is invisible.

Third-person POV: John hit him. This POV is common in commercial fiction.

Omniscient POV: In this POV the author is in the sky looking down and can write what anyone in the story is thinking and can shift from one POV to another. Because of this, it is easy for a reader to get confused unless the POV is handled well by the writer.

Warning: Avoid shifting the POV from a central character to minor characters. It will only complicate or confuse the reader's experience.

The nuances surrounding the complex subject of point of view are covered in depth in chapter 13 of *Stein on Writing*. For switching from one POV to another within a story, I believe in a simple solution: In my novel *The Magician* I start out with a narrator's point of view of a town and introduce the main character, a sixteen-year-old named Ed Japhet. On page 6 I make the first switch from the narrator's point of view to that of a character:

COMMENT BY HIS FATHER
(Terence Japhet, age 46, teacher)

On page 7 the father's comment is interrupted by:

COMMENT BY HIS GIRLFRIEND
(Lila Hurst, age 16, student)

On page 8 I switch to another first-person point of view:

COMMENT BY DR. GUNTHER KOCH
(Manhattan psychiatrist, age 57)

The Magician was published in 1971 and received excellent reviews. Not once did I hear an objection from any reviewer, teacher of writing, or reader to this simple method of switching the point of view to another character. If you like it, try it; one can't copyright an idea and I am glad to share with you my shortcut to getting inside another character's point of view.

Point of View (More)

Have you ever tried writing from the point of view of the antagonist in a story? If not, try doing so as an exercise to determine why the antagonist is the way he is.

Point of View, Shifting

In my novel *Other People,* each chapter is headed by the name of a major character whose point of view is used in that chapter. No critic has ever objected to that procedure.

Preaching

Banish preaching from fiction unless coming from the mouth of a character who is a pastor. It is better for points to be derived from the events and dialogue of a story. In nonfiction, conclusions gracefully put will sound informative rather than preachy.

Precision

One of the marks of an accomplished writer is the selection of words that provide a precise meaning. The obstacle to overcome is oneself; all of us in putting words to paper habitually use words that are not precise because with few exceptions that's what we do when we talk. We provide information "off the top of the head," words that come first. In addition to precision, freshness in the choice of words is important. For example, Martin Amis comes up with a word that is both precise and fresh in the first sentence of his essay "The Second Plane" in the book of the same name. He is describing a moment in what we have come to call 9/11, the destruction of the twin towers in Manhattan by Islamist terrorists. Amis writes, "It was the advent of the second plane, sharking in low over the Statue of Liberty: that was the defining moment." The word I admire is "sharking." For those of us who saw the second plane fly into the South Tower, the word "sharking" is exactly right. It is also fresh because this form of the word "shark" is archaic and comes across as new yet accurate. "Sharking" once stood for a negative activity, like loan sharking. Amis has given us a word that pictures the plane in the moments before impact. In the same essay, Amis uses the word "bipolar" to good effect. The word is usually used to describe a psychiatric disorder characterized by alternating episodes of mania and depression, highs and lows. Amis carries the word to a new dimension when in the same essay he is talking about the West confronting an irrational, agonistic, theocratic system that is unappeasably opposed to the West's existence. He says, "The world suddenly feels bipolar." It is both accurate and fresh.

A literary writer invents appropriate uses for words that are not commonplace.

Precision and Freshness in Public Speaking

Some writers are shy and duck opportunities to speak to audiences about their written work. But for those who are not, it pays to think of words and phrases that might be enjoyed by an audience that may thereby be tempted to savor the author's work. When I think of speakers who can delight audiences, I immediately remember two who couldn't have been more different from each other, though both were British in origin.

I was David Frost's first American publisher during his heyday, and he had two abilities that helped him sell a lot of his books. He had a phenomenal memory for the names of people he met in passing, and he had an arsenal of quick comments whenever he was invited to talk. My favorite of the latter always came at the end when the audience applauded. He would say, "Thank you for your support; I will always wear it." For reasons beyond description here, it always worked, which is why one of my colleagues was delegated to remind him before a talk that he had already used that for a particular audience, because such phrases draw a negative response if heard for the second time.

Harold Macmillan, once the head of a distinguished British publishing firm and prime minister of his country, was a master of public speaking. Most such speeches are written. And edited. And rewritten if the speech is important. Macmillan when at a lectern or similar prop played with words and phrases for maximum audience impact. Believe me, those words were written and rewritten and polished to perfection, but they were delivered in an offhand manner, as if he were speaking extemporaneously. The professional writer will examine his text as carefully as a speechmaker might to make certain he has the best word in every instance. Look for two things: clarity and precision. The mot juste means the exactly right word. The degree to which you scan your work to determine that you have the best words in the best order is often the mark of your professionalism, particularly if you are a freelance writer. Don't depend on the editor. My friend James Baldwin became a successful public speaker during the 1960s; he spoke from a carefully written and rewritten text but made it seem as if he had just thought of the wording.

Prologues

Some professional readers of fiction (agents, editors, marketing people) skip prologues when considering a novel. If the prologue to a novel contains essential information for understanding the narrative that follows, consider ways of conveying that information in the opening chapter. A brief prologue may be used in nonfiction if it serves the purpose of opening the door to the book in an enticing way.

Punctuation

In fiction you are creating an experience for the reader, most often in the form of a visible scene with one or more characters doing something. Punctuation can sometimes get in the way of that experience. I seldom use colons, semicolons, or dashes in fiction. Commas can help create the rhythm of a sentence.

R

Readers

If you are writing fiction, the primary objective of your work is to provide the reader with an experience. In narrative nonfiction, you are providing factual information to the reader's imagination. When writing for theater or film, you are providing an experience to people in an audience, who often react to a line of dialogue, particularly comic dialogue, as if they were all one. The reader of a newspaper is often skimming for a headline or a photograph that will arouse his or her curiosity or interest or to find a familiar section or columnist. It serves a writer well to think from time to time of what his customer is hoping for.

Reading

Is this reaching you too late? Reading is not an elective for someone who hopes one day to be a published writer. You can't become an astronomer without a sun, moon, and stars, and a curiosity about what goes on up there. A tailor who doesn't wear clothes is an anomaly. When younger (ah!) I occasionally met a writer who did very little reading. That bothered me until I realized that the person I'd been worried about was probably not a writer. A swimmer has to get wet. A writer must soak himself in stories, books, and plays from an early age so that he can backstroke and sidestroke in a difficult craft. Youth is the time that the habit of books becomes an addiction that, unlike tobacco, is life enhancing.

Be careful of what you read. If you read summertime novels on the beach and enjoy them, it may become what you will write.

Reading for Screenwriters

Adventures in the Screen Trade by William Goldman is a book that you will probably read twice, once for the fun of getting to know a difficult industry and a second time to mark passages you'll want to reread from time to time.

Reading Other Writers

When you are reading nonfiction and come across a sentence or a paragraph that is particularly well crafted, reexamining it at once may provide a technique that you can use. Don't trust your memory. Make a note of it, preferably in a nearby notebook devoted to the recording of such craft points.

However, in the case of fiction, if you are experiencing the story you may not want to interrupt that experience, which is why I read stories and novels with Post-its handy so that I can mark the place and come back to what I liked when no longer in thrall to the story. This helps keep you as a reader rather than a writer who is reading for pointers.

Realism and Fantasy in Drama

In Shakespeare, even the realistic plays or parts of plays have an ingredient that isn't a duplication of reality, because the plays were written in verse. In the early 1930s realism swept through theater and many plays were made to seem like slices of real life. Then a few dramatists invented a different kind of theater: Bertolt Brecht's *Mother Courage and Her Children* is an example of a play with political intent in an avant-garde form. Edward Albee brought silences and repetition into theater.

Realism in Fiction

Realism, developed in the nineteenth century, claimed a major place in fiction. Theodore Dreiser is an example of a realistic writer whose use of words was "lifelike" but lacked lift and resonance. Saul Bellow said Dreiser was a natural, a primitive, but that Dreiser's work had elements of genius despite his clumsiness.

Real People in Fiction

This is tricky. Brief parts, especially without dialogue, can be useful. I used to edit a tremendously successful suspense novelist whose work occasionally had a background character like Winston Churchill momentarily visible. The big danger is giving real people words to speak.

Rebirth of Abandoned Manuscripts

The best case history I know of is Mark Twain's. He was about halfway through *Tom Sawyer,* page 400 according to his account, when the air went out of the balloon. (Four hundred pages in those days would be far fewer on today's computerized pages.) He couldn't write a line more. He was surprised, distressed, and disappointed in himself. "The tank had run dry" was his assessment. He knew he still had half the book to write, but it was no use. He put the manuscript aside.

Two years later he took the manuscript out and read the last chapter that he had written. His imagination varoomed. He discovered that when the tank runs dry and you leave it alone, it will fill up again in time. It intruded on his sleep and work while what he called "this unconscious and profitable cerebration" was going on. He had plenty of material now, and he finished *Tom Sawyer* without a touch of trouble. Later, the same kind of thing happened with some of his other works.

At about the time that I learned what Mark Twain had done, I passed by a cardboard box in which I had stowed about half of a nonfiction manuscript I had abandoned years earlier for reasons I can't for the life of me remember. I read it in a glow and couldn't wait to get back to finish it. We are all guilty of abandonment, which may require later rescue. Shredders are not suitable storage places for temporarily orphaned manuscripts.

Recommended Reading for Writers

Literary fiction: *The Stories of John Cheever* by John Cheever.

Historical fiction: *Disraeli in Love* by Maurice Edelman.

Thriller: The first chapter of John le Carré's *The Spy Who Came In from the Cold*. If you read the novel a long time ago, read the first chapter again. And again until you understand how suspense can be created.

Biography: *Isaiah Berlin: A Life* by Michael Ignatieff; *Three Who Made a Revolution* by Bertram D. Wolfe.

Reference: For nonfiction writers *The People's Chronology: A Year-by-Year Record of Human Events from Prehistory to the Present* by James Trager. My 1979 copy is 1,206 pages. The book has been revised since. My copy weighs three and a half pounds but somehow feels heavier than a young child. With the present availability of information on Wikipedia or through Google and other search engines, huge volumes of fact seem unnecessary. Wrong. The book has a marvelous advantage for writers because you can open it at random and come upon historical facts you would not have known to look up on a search engine. It's a lift for the imagination. It gives you things to think about that weren't in your head. There's enough in this volume to throw at a burglar or to stimulate even a drowsy imagination. The downside is that even used copies are expensive, possibly because smart people won't part with theirs.

Another hefty volume you can use in a nearby library and think about buying when you've struck publishing gold. It's known as the *LMP*, which stands for *Literary Market Place*. It comes in two volumes. Volume 1 lists publishers, literary agents, editorial services, trade associations, book trade courses, awards and prizes, and books and magazines for the publishing trade. You get the key names spelled correctly, addresses (including e-mail), phone and fax numbers. Volume 2, not sold separately, includes this information for book review media, public relations firms, book clubs, manufacturers, distributors, consultants, employment agencies, translators, and various artists and art services. I have more than twenty Post-its stuck on pages of volume 1, which means it's been useful to me. All that's required is to avoid luxuries for a month because these two volumes come as a set and are expensive. They are updated annually.

When you're in the middle of writing and suddenly feel like a pricked balloon, vacant, not sure of where to go next, here's a quick solution. Open a large dictionary at random. Check out each defined word on the left-hand page, then the right-hand page, pronouncing each word (to yourself so you don't get carried away literally!). Just looking one by one at the defined words, you'll be surprised at the number of times your mind will switch on and provide a memory that may fit the need in your writing.

Even more useful than a dictionary is a thesaurus. My most frequently used reference book is The *Oxford American Writer's Thesaurus,* which provides synonyms, antonyms, and word spectrums that show shadings of meaning between two polar opposites such as "rude" and "polite" "failure" and "failure"and "success." It's a good way of getting rid of repetition, learning precision, and stimulating your brain. It also can make your writing more interesting by providing more exact words and different words than you customarily use.

The *Oxford American Writer's Thesaurus* is not expensive for its size and is of great value to writers of both fiction and nonfiction for finding the exact word you need. Its magic is in the concept. It takes you from one extreme to its opposite, step by step. Here's an example:

▶ *rude*

insolent	short	civil
churlish	sharp	courteous
contumelious	uncharitable	diplomatic
ill-mannered	unchivalrous	respectful
bad-mannered	unpleasant	well-mannered
offensive	disagreeable	polished
insulting	discourteous	considerate
abusive	disrespectful	deferential
derogatory	presumptuous	proper
disparaging	impertinent	gracious
underbred	impudent	formal
malapert	cheeky	refined
ill-bred	audacious	genteel
ungallant	uncivil	well brought up
ungentlemanly	uncomplimentary	well-bred
unladylike	tactless	mannerly
unmannerly	mannerless	cultured
uncouth	undiplomatic	cultivated
ungracious		sophisticated
graceless	**offhand**	urbane
impolite		elegant
crass	conscientious	courtly
curt	well-behaved	ladylike
brusque	thoughtful	gentlemanly
brash	tactful	chivalrous
blunt	discreet	gallant

▶ *polite* ◀

A book that I refer to less frequently is a *recent* slang dictionary. I can't recommend *The Dictionary of Contemporary Slang* because Stein and Day published it in 1984, and believe me slang changes fast. However, an old slang dictionary can be of benefit if you are writing about a prior time, unless you are writing solely about people who wouldn't be caught dead using slang.

Essay: "Why I Write" and "Shooting an Elephant" and others by George Orwell. I would also suggest two anthologies: *The Art of the Personal Essay* selected and with an introduction by Phillip Lopate and *The Oxford Book of Essays* edited by John Gross, which includes James Thurber's "My Own Ten Rules for a Happy Marriage."

Repetition

Chances are a teacher told you to avoid repetition. Here's an example to the contrary.

> When Warren came that day to the door of the house on California Street Charlotte did not answer.
> When Warren telephoned Charlotte hung up.
> When Warren stood on the sidewalk outside the house on California Street at two A.M. and threw stones at the windows Charlotte closed the shutters.

The example is from a novel called *A Book of Common Prayer* by Joan Didion. If you have Joan Didion's talent, you can use repetition any time you think it works. Moreover, Didion has dropped some commas that your teacher would have wanted you to put in. Art breaks rules.

Resonance

This is an important subject for writers whose aspirations are literary. Resonance can contribute much to nonfiction (see the Bertram Wolfe example below). In fiction resonance supplies what lift does for an airplane. *Moby-Dick* has instant resonance in its first words: "Call me Ishmael." The biblical association provides the lift. T. Coraghessan Boyle's 1987 novel *World's End* evokes death: "The day was typical of April in the vale of the Hudson—raw and drizzling, the earth exhaling vapor as if it were breathing its last." Resonance creates lift. This complex subject is treated at much greater length in chapter 31 of *Stein on Writing*.

V. S. Naipaul provides resonance in the first sentence of his novel *A Bend in the River:* "The world is what it is; men who are nothing, who allow themselves to become nothing, have no place in it."

The second sentence is where a lesser writer might have started the novel: "Nazruddin, who had sold me the shop cheap, didn't think I would have it easy when I took over."

The ideal resonance derives from the writing itself. My mentor in this was Bertram Wolfe, whose masterpiece, *Three Who Made a Revolution,* has sold many hundreds of thousands of copies in English. Would that all historians wrote as well. I learned much from editing the later work of this master. Here's how *Three Who Made a Revolution* starts, a model for nonfiction.

> *The great Eurasian Plain opposes few obstacles to frost and wind and drought, to migrant hordes and marching armies. In earlier*

centuries the plain was dominated by vast Asiatic empires, Iranian, Turkish, Mongolian. As the last of these melted away, Moscovy expanded to take their place, expanded steadily through several centuries until it became the largest continuous land empire in the world. Like the tide over limitless flats, it spread with elemental force over an endless stretch of forest and steppe, sparsely settled by backward nomadic peoples. Wherever it met resistance, it would pause as the tide does to gather head, then resume its inexorable advance. Only at the distant margins does the plateau end in great mountain barriers: the snowy summits of the Caucasus; the Pamirs, roof of the world—where two of our three protagonists have peaks named in their honor, thrusting up over four miles each into the sky; the Altai, Sayan and Stanovoi mountains forming China's natural wall. How could a people not be great and not aspire to greatness, whose horizon was as unlimited as their Eurasian Plain?

The visual sweep introduces a work of history with resonance that stems from the skill of the writing. It is not too much for a beginner to hope for; I've read the work of relative beginners whose work already displays tufts of resonance.

Look at the first sentence of what you are now writing. Does it have lift, resonance? Is there something you might say first, a sentence, a thought that would settle an editor in a chair, happily ready to read what follows because he is in the hands of a gifted writer?

Revision

I despair when I see a young writer lightly touching up a first draft in preparation for sending it out to the world. Revision, especially of fiction, is a serious and prolonged process of perfecting draft after draft. New writers, exposed to editorial advice in workshops, classes, and books, often don't know some of the shortcuts for revision developed by their predecessors. Hemingway wrote the last chapter of *A Farewell to Arms* 119 times. You won't if you learn to use the lockstitch technique. It comes from sewing. For every stitch you take you go back a little ways into the previous stitch, and that's exactly how I manage my novels. Each morning when I sit down at the computer I go back over the last few pages written the day before. I sometimes strengthen those pages in minor ways and then continue. The lockstitch technique helps continuity. It jump-starts your work for the day and gets you going in the flow of your storytelling. You'll find that when you get to that last chapter, you'll have a better idea of what to do because of your earlier lockstitching. You'll also find yourself writing much stronger finales.

You're welcome.

When you're ready to write a wholly new draft of your manuscript, time is your best friend. Let the manuscript cool off for a few days, or preferably longer. This will increase your distance from what you wrote in the earlier draft and will make revision more productive.

For book-length manuscripts, fixing major problems first is a time-saver. As you move along in a draft you may come upon a problem that will cause revision in other chapters, possibly earlier chapters. But you've already revised them! Hence, fix major problems that involve other chapters first, then go into a revision of consecutive chapters.

Every book-length manuscript has a weakest chapter. Cut it if you can. Don't worry, you'll still have a weakest chapter.

Once you can do this without undue pain, you'll find yourself strengthening your book every time you use this discipline.

Now for a giant step the majority of writers don't use, to their detriment. For both fiction and nonfiction, revision can be more effective if a draft is revised *in a different medium*. For instance, if the manuscript was written on computer, ideally it should be examined and revised by its author in hard copy, printed on paper. True, the inputting of corrections made on paper into the computer requires additional work. If you're a productive professional writer, you may find it a worthwhile—and tax-deductible—expenditure if hard-copy improvements can be input by someone else. The fewer times the author is exposed to his own drafts, the fresher he will be as a reviser of his work.

Plays, screenplays, and scenes in fiction containing significant dialogue might be recorded by a person *other than the author* on any kind of recording device, in a monotone, unobserved by the author. The author can later listen to the recording and detect flaws in the dialogue that might not be caught on the page.

There, you have learned some big steps toward improving anything you write. You're welcome, but do take a look at **Line-Editing** in this book, because it's frequently misunderstood.

S

Scene
A unit of writing within a larger work, a scene is not a short story because it is almost always a link in a chain of scenes in a play or film or novel. Each scene within a larger work has the obligation to carry the story forward. It is useful to conclude scenes with a suspenseful or surprising turn of events to thrust the reader into the scene that follows. Advice worth remembering: *Never take the reader where the reader wants to go.*

A scene ideally should arouse an emotional experience for the viewer or reader. In a novel, which tends to have many more scenes than a play, the process of revision should involve the elimination of scenes that are weak and hurt their neighboring scenes.

Scene Inspiration and Instruction
Writers of fiction who map out their entire story in advance may need to heed this recommendation as much as the novelist who experiences the sudden void of not being sure of what should come next. It's even an aid for writers who've mapped their entire story and suddenly find they've written a scene that isn't good enough. The book I'm recommending might be useful when you're first making the map that you will follow. I'm speaking about the absolutely most helpful inspiration for scene planning, a book that I have been through countless times. It is Barnaby Conrad's *101 Best Scenes Ever Written*, where most of the examples are from fine literature.

Instruction books are rarely entertaining as well as inspiring, but this one is and can kick a writer's imagination into high gear in seconds. You'll find scenes from Ernest Hemingway, Tennessee Williams, Jack London, John Steinbeck, Leo Tolstoy, Evelyn Waugh, Sinclair Lewis, Orson Welles, James M. Cain, Erich Maria Remarque, Elmore Leonard, Daniel Defoe, Mark Twain, Alexandre Dumas, Graham Greene, Edgar Rice Burroughs, Somerset Maugham, and Noël Coward. You'll also be encouraged to find mistakes some of the giants made—and rectified.

Screenplay Technique in Fiction
Consider an example from the experience of Leslie Fiedler. He was best known as a literary critic, and thought to be the successor to Edmund Wilson. In addition to his literary criticism, Fiedler wrote a few novels and had a novelist's special interest in film. In one novel, there was to be a very short scene of great importance based on action involving three people in just a few seconds. A person in the story is coming out of the back door of a house carrying a baseball. He throws it to a second person just as a third person roars off on a motorcycle. Try as Fiedler might, this action scene, important to the novel, wasn't working until he imagined the action as it would be photographed for film. We see the person coming out of the door and then throwing the ball, see the ball in flight, and then see the person catching it. In other words, three shots for a simple action, but during the third part, the catch, we hear the sound of one of the people roaring off on his motorcycle. As the ball is caught there is the sound of a crash. What we've done is break up a brief

scene that didn't work when *told* but, when *shown* in three parts as it would be filmed, the action came alive to the reader.

Screenwriting

Those who are experienced in writing screenplays as well as fiction might argue that writing a screenplay is not writing as it is generally conceived. Screenplays are instructions for the director and others involved in making what will be seen, except for the dialogue, which, if done well, can be readable, although a screenplay as a whole is usually difficult and unenjoyable for the lay reader.

Next to having a computer program geared for screenwriting with its unusual formats, a beginner in screenwriting needs to know quite a bit about how Hollywood functions and behaves. I had the lucky opportunity of turning several screenplays into fiction so they could be read by laymen. While Elia Kazan was filming *America America* abroad, it fell to Patricia Day as his friend, editor, and publisher to turn the screenplay into readable fiction. The film was, of course, nominated for many awards, and the book, to my and Kazan's surprise, sold a few million copies. Kazan's story for the film was exciting but, with the paraphernalia of film, not readily readable by laymen. The transformation task—film script into fiction—was repeated several times, notably Eleanor Perry's script for John Cheever's "The Swimmer," Dylan Thomas's "The Beach at Falesa," and Sinclair Lewis and Dore Schary's collaboration, "Storm in the West." I believe that despite the very high standing of Dore Schary in the film business and Sinclair Lewis's reputation as a writer, the film was never made, but the book was read. Novel writing and film writing are different species. The dialogue differs only in that in novel form the characters speak in the reader's brain and in film the dialogue is spoken by actors.

Segue

Originally used in music to connote movement from one theme to another. The emphasis is on the smoothness of the change. That meaning comes over into writing both fiction and nonfiction. See **Backstory** for its uses.

Self-Confidence

Occasionally an adult who is not an experienced writer will think he can write a story or even a novel because he's been reading other people's writing and has come to believe that he can do the same. He overlooks the fact that writing fiction or nonfiction is a highly disciplined craft that can take years to master. He's heard stories, he's read stories—why not try to write one? If you've taken an airplane many times why not fly one? The truth, coming from someone who has done both, is that learning to fly safely is less complex and quicker than learning to write a story that will engage the imaginations of thousands of people. Inspiration is a quite small part of the process. Most of it is hard work. You are operating on the brains and imaginations of people you have never met who live in France or Russia or Timbuktu. A good novel will often be translated into other languages. It will be read by people of many ages and characteristics. It's a big responsibility not to be taken lightly, and the key may be to think of it as engineering *the* words. My dictionary says that engineering is "the application of scientific and mathematical principles to practical ends such as the design, manufacture, and operation of efficient and economical structures, machines, processes, and systems." Yep, that's writing.

Senses

The senses are all stimuli for the reader and can heighten the reality of a scene in fiction or narrative. It is odd how often four of the six senses of mankind are forgotten as writers focus on what is seen or heard. Surely, one feels a strong handshake and smells food, appetizing and delicious. A meal should not be bypassed without a sense of how the food tasted or smelled. Taste or smell can be important for a story; remember Proust's madeleine? (My father made me aware of wordplay by his usual answer when folks asked him, "How do you feel?" His answer was "With my hands.") His firm handshake was memorable, though not quite as strong as the handshake of a workman I know whose friendly grip put my right hand out of activity for more than a week. The senses are all stimuli for the reader and can heighten the reality of a scene in fiction or narrative, as I hope I have just done.

Sentence Length

It takes years of writing and revising carefully to be able to hear the music of sentences. It also requires an appreciation of fine writing in other people's books and a lot of experience in reading writers who put sentences together well. Those are generalities. How can I be of help?

I can tell you that varying sentence length is the norm, and no particular formula works. For instance, the last sentence has two clauses that total sixteen words. The sentence before that has six words. The sentence that precedes that one has only three words. I had no idea of the word count of each sentence either before or after writing it. I was listening for the sound of the sentence, what I call its music. In fiction particularly, the range of sentence length can be greater.

In the novel I am currently finishing, with about 70,000 words done, my computer advises me of the following statistics: The average word length is 4.5 letters. That seems short but allows for the many words we use of 1, 2, and 3 letters. I am also told that I average 12 words per sentence. My longest sentence is 181, and if I find it I will see if I can't cut it in half. The important statistic is the average word length. Checking those numbers against a current nonfiction book I'm writing, both the average word length and the average number of words per sentence is greater, but the longest sentence in the nonfiction book is half the length of the one in fiction. What I gleaned from this exercise is the variety of word length one employs if you are concerned about the sound of those sentences when spoken aloud. If even a small part of a manuscript doesn't *sound* right to you after you've let the manuscript lie fallow for a while, check to see if it needs revision or cutting.

Sentimentality

A trap to be avoided. Emotion is what a writer creates in a reader, a strong feeling that may be good or bad. A mistake often made is to tell the reader directly about what a character is feeling, which can have the opposite effect or no effect. Telling the reader a child is crying may produce sympathy, but it will be a cold conclusion without feeling. If a child is biting its lip trying not to cry, you're getting closer to generating an emotion in the reader. If the child opens its mouth to protest again and again and no words come out, you've got a child the reader can begin to empathize with. Indirectness works better than directness when emotions are involved. If an elderly woman is coming out of the doctor's office into the waiting room biting her lower lip the reader will empathize without your having to say that she got bad news. Sentimentality, crude telling of an emotion, often has the opposite effect.

Settings

In the nineteenth century many writers would design a setting in detail, but seldom doing more for the senses than a stage set empty of actors. Of course characters must not be let loose in the atmosphere. They need to be planted in a specific place, which might well be described by one or two of its dominant features because readers today are in more of a hurry.

A setting ideally should be meaningful in the story and by its difference entice the reader's curiosity. An ordinary setting is a lazy waste of words.

Tip: Sometimes another character's interior view of the protagonist—even if it's a mistaken and hostile view—can accomplish more than working from within the protagonist's mind.

Sex Scenes

I dislike passing the buck, but if you're going to have a sex scene in your novel, I highly recommend your acquiring and reading twice a book called *The Joy of Writing Sex* by Elizabeth Benedict, which covers the subject wittily. Benedict, the author of four novels, has taught fiction writing at Princeton, Swarthmore, the Iowa Writers' Workshop, and the New School in New York. She points out that sex is not an ATM withdrawal and that while your characters don't have to speak, don't forget that they can. If you are squeamish, you have been warned. And if you're squeamish, you can always write a sex scene that takes place back a century or two. Fiction is usually about somebody wanting something very much. Sex—or the absence of it—would seem to fall into that category. Look at sex not as pornography but as a disclosure of character.

There's also a book called *Snoopy's Guide to the Writing Life* that was edited by Barnaby Conrad, one of the great writing teachers of his time (and the author of a mere thirty books), with Monte Schulz, son of Snoopy's inventor, Charles Schulz. The book, now out of print though available in the used-book market, contains short sections on a variety of writing subjects by a lot of bestselling writers. I was assigned three pages on the subject of sex scenes not because I have seven children but because the information was lifted—I hasten to say with permission—from *Stein on Writing*.

Here's a hint: a good sex scene is not primarily about the sex.

Short Advice from the Masters Amended

Samuel Johnson: "The only end of writing is to enable the reader better to enjoy life, or better to endure it." What about groceries?

James Joyce: "To live, to err, to fall, to triumph, to recreate life out of life!" To be made of rubber?

Norman Mailer: "The first art work in an artist is the shaping of his own personality." Mailer followed his advice by shaping his pugnacious personality. I once edited a short piece that Mailer wrote for a friend's book and Mailer was a pussycat about my editing.

"Show, Don't Tell" in Fiction

This frequent admonition relates to the common error of telling what happened rather than showing it happening. The writer of short stories or novels is urged to make action visible to the reader as if it were happening before his eyes. **Backstory** (which see) works best if it is shown rather than described. This does not relate to quick references to the past, for example as in, "You never told me the truth of where you'd been," or "I'll never forget the time you tried to carry it yourself," or "A long time ago they'd arranged the comfortable armchairs and the sofa in their living room ready for conversation among guests and friends." These examples don't switch the reader to a scene in the past.

"Show, Don't Tell" in Nonfiction

Readers brought up on movies and television are used to *seeing*. In journalism and other nonfiction writing, the emphasis should be on keeping information as visual as possible. Relevant details of dress, body movement, and speech and details of the environment all help the reader see what's happening.

Showing and Telling

One of the most common craft suggestions writers hear from their teachers or elders is to show rather than tell as often as they can, but what's usually missing is an explanation of why. I have it on good authority that people remember approximately 20 percent of what they hear, 70 percent of what they see, but 90 percent of what they both see and hear. You hear the words that you read but if you also are seeing what is happening, the combination of senses provides a more memorable experience! For the basics, see **Emotion.** For showing through dialogue, see **Dialogue, Advanced.**

Simple Character Solutions

Complex characters are usually more interesting than characters with simple attributes, but your work will be more interesting if even the most minor character is different from what the reader would expect. One way of dealing with the matter is to consider opposites. For instance, greeting your protagonist at the door of the house he wants to enter is a very old man. If all we know about the character is that he's very old, that will bring out our sympathy but may not bring the character to life. Therefore try the opposite. Your protagonist is at the door, which is answered by an old man who sniffs several times without reaching for a handkerchief and says, "Whatja want?" Your protagonist says, "Is this the Larsen house?"

"Nah," says the old man.

"Does the Larsen family live on this block?"

"How the hell should I know?"

"Is there anyone else at home who might know?"

"Nah!" He slams the door shut.

You haven't created the stereotypical old man. Do you want to humanize him?

He can say, "I don't know nobody."

"I'm sorry."

"You look sorry. Step back, I'm closing the door."

Slang

Colloquialisms or contemporary street language can lighten dialogue in fiction but can also be a hazard to all but those who've heard the words before. A glitch is anything that makes the reader see words on a page, that takes the novel reader momentarily out of the experience. If you want to introduce slang, try to use expressions that have been around for a while, which will make it more likely that readers will know the expression and not stop to puzzle over the word. There are several sites on the Internet that specialize in slang, some mired in very new and uninteresting sex slang. You might do better with a slang dictionary published some years earlier so the words are likely to be familiar to more readers and not an obstacle to experience. In most cases a good thesaurus is useful for finding colloquial expressions that are accurate and likely to be known by readers.

Social Class in Fiction

It was critic Lionel Trilling who emphasized that social class might well be the most important element in fiction. That was true of much nineteenth-century fiction, and remains true even in allegedly classless societies. Social class can immediately set up delicate or strong barriers between strangers. Even vestiges of class can stimulate conflict between husband and wife, among children or adults in neighborhoods, among business and professional people, and between layers within professions and occupations.

Social Class in Nonfiction

Class can have a powerful effect if the writer thinks about the possibilities. In introducing a person, an item of clothing such as a cap worn with the bill in the back can establish class, as can a woman's manner of dress. An action such as chewing gum can also suggest social rank. Politicians betray their social class by their words or actions. For example, "The Senator spoke as if the words originated not in his mind but on the typed notes he'd conspicuously put on the lectern."

Sounds Wrong

We're talking about something in a draft of your fiction, journalism, or other nonfiction that on rereading doesn't sound right. That's not very precise but experienced writers will know what I'm talking about: Your experience in writing and in life comes to your rescue when you detect something is not quite right in context. If you're in a hurry and react by thinking, *The hell with it, it doesn't matter,* believe me, it does matter because a flaw in good writing may be only a few words but it can make a difference in the reader's attitude toward the entire article, chapter, book. I've heard resistance in the form of "It doesn't matter, I just want to get it done and over," or "I haven't got the time." If that's your attitude you are turning "Whoa" into "Woe." Sometimes that feeling is caused by a word or phrase that is inexact in context or that strays from your intention. It can also be caused by an unnecessary sentence or paragraph that snuck in while you were typing fast. Perhaps you should reread **Glitch.** If you get into the habit of listening for anything off-key and fixing it, you will thank me for it.

Stein's Prescriptions

Number 1 has been quoted in Elia Kazan's autobiography: $1 + 1 = \frac{1}{2}$. What that means is that saying something twice is less forceful than saying it once.

My second prescription is newer, for writers who use computers (who doesn't?) and work on more than one project or manuscript at a time. Most of us do drafts of our work and sometimes confuse which draft we are working on. One can, of course, give each new draft a number and a date. However, sometimes material is grafted from one draft to another for a variety of reasons—a jolt of electricity, a distracting phone call, a doorbell, a sudden need, a visitor. And computers are delicate creatures and sometimes shut down or create mayhem for no particular reason. As a countermove I use a very simple system to keep control of my drafts. After I save a draft, I note *the date and the number of words.* Computers are able to give you an accurate word count in a second. It is a great way to identify the current manuscript if you have more than one draft. It creates a ping of pleasure to learn that I will be working on the right draft whose word length is correct.

Stereotypes

The use of hackneyed plots and the creation of stock characters are two of the worst faults of fiction writers, especially in so-called commercial fiction, which won't be at all commercial until the writers learn to think anew when developing characters and stories. Formulaic stories do not provide the reader with an experience that is fresh and newly pleasurable. The detective can be the same but unless you're wearing Conan Doyle's shoes, the detective's adversary should be surprisingly new and put a fresh face on the story.

Story Progression

Neither fiction nor narrative nonfiction requires *logical* progression from paragraph to paragraph, scene to scene, or chapter to chapter. A story must evoke the reader's curiosity. The writer as architect may have a building plan. The writer as bricklayer lures the reader from page to page by postponing information and by producing surprises. Surprise is a special benefit of reading. Creating it is part of the author's work.

Straying

This isn't about conjugal loyalty; it's about straying from your métier. Some excellent journalists and nonfiction writers stumble when they first try their hand at fiction. But even within fiction it can be unwise to stray. I thought John le Carré's spy novels were excellently crafted thrillers. Then he wrote a novel-length love story. I was not the only publisher who was offered it and declined. Eventually it was published and crashed. He dutifully went back to espionage and he returned to the world as a winner. This is not a moral lesson, it is a business lesson. Stray at your own risk from what you do best.

Stream of Consciousness
A continuous and silent unraveling of thoughts that entered into fiction at about the same time as psychoanalysis came into vogue. James Joyce was the outstanding early practitioner. Joyce progressed from the stories and memoirlike fiction to his masterwork *Ulysses,* which emboldened other writers to try their hand at the streaming of words. Tip: Joyce's ambitious last work, *Finnegans Wake,* in which the end flows into the beginning, makes sense if read aloud with an Irish accent.

Strength (in Writing)
See **Verbs.**

Stressing the Reader
See **Tension** and **Suspense in Fiction** and **Suspense in Nonfiction.**

Strong Characters
Men and women who are fierce about achieving something against high odds.

Stuck?

Open your dictionary at random and skim the facing pages until you see a word you are pretty sure you have never used before. Make up a sentence that includes that word, any sentence about anything. Look at that sentence. Do you like the sound of the word? How might you use it in your novel? Could you use it in an e-mail to a friend? Turn to a good thesaurus (if you don't own a good thesaurus that you use often, you are not yet a wordsmith) and look at synonyms for that word. Is there a synonym that you like better? Can you use it in the same sentence instead of the word you originally picked? If you're still stuck—I'm sorry—turn the pages of your thesaurus slowly, reading every word until you find one that you can use where you were when you got stuck.

Style

A distinctive style can be an asset, for example Hemingway's, but imitative styles lessen the appreciation of your work, as does a highly eccentric style that may interfere with the reader's experience. Gertrude Stein (no relation) is known for sentences like "A rose is a rose is a rose" but any attempt at imitation with things other than a rose would impede the reader's experience and would be counterproductive. Style also involves matters other than wordplay—for instance, one character in first person deriding the character of another to the reader.

If you read your own work carefully, you may find that you do some things a certain way more often than you are aware of. If it works for the narrative, that's fine. If it obtrudes and lessens the effect of the story, it's time to rectify the habit. Nothing obtrudes in a narrative as much as a forced or contrived style.

Subject Matter

One of the acknowledged great writers of his time, Gabriel García Márquez, is usually praised for his imaginative writing, but he has said quite clearly that there's not a line in his work that doesn't have a basis in reality. You look at an airplane on the ground and wonder, how could such a large and weighty machine stuffed with people be lifted up in the air? The most prosaic subject matter can have lift with a little help from your experience or imagination.

Surprises

Readers of fiction enjoy surprises, for instance a character suddenly acting uncharacteristically that effects a change. Even changes in small matters add life to a character, particularly if toward the end the reader is aware of a character's change in more important matters. The legitimacy of big surprises must be planted ahead of time.

Suspense in Fiction

Suspense is the ingredient that compels the reader to continue reading, to continue on the story's journey and find out what happens. Reminder: If at the end of a chapter the reader is anxious to see a door opened, don't open the door at the beginning of the next chapter; go somewhere else, leaving the reader in suspense. *Never take the reader where the reader wants to go.*

Suspense in Nonfiction

Some nonfiction writers have a notion that suspense is solely for writers of fiction. Some assume that what is interesting in their work is the subject matter, so maintaining the reader's interest through suspense is unnecessary. That view is mistaken unless the writer is willing to have the reader skim his work looking for nuggets of information. If the writer wants his work read and talked about, he will learn the techniques necessary to keep the reader reading through suspense. Consider a book on a very serious topic indeed, Richard Rhodes's *The Making of the Atomic Bomb*. Here is the book's first paragraph:

> *In London, where Southampton Row passes Russell Square, across from the British Museum in Bloomsbury, Leo Szilard waited irritably one gray Depression morning for the stoplight to change. A trace of rain had fallen during the night; Tuesday, September 12, 1933, dawned cool, humid and dull. Drizzling rain would begin again in early afternoon. When Szilard told the story later he never mentioned his destination that morning. He may have had none; he often walked to think. In any case another destination intervened. The stoplight changed to green. Szilard stepped off the curb. As he crossed the street time cracked open before him and he saw a way to the future, death into the world and all our woe, the shape of things to come.*

Notice the particularity: uncomfortable weather, the middle of the Great Depression, a man deep in thought while walking, and then an illumination of a discovery that was to change the future of the world. The reader must guess at the thought that occurred to Szilard at that moment. You have witnessed suspense in action, the providing of information that is also the holding off of information that now becomes a necessity to the reader, the answer waiting for him in the paragraphs to come.

Rhodes's book won the Pulitzer Prize, the National Book Award, and the National Book Critics Circle Award. Like a novel, it starts out with a character, a person hurrying—to what destination? What is this about? The reader is not entirely unknowing—he knows the title of the book, he may have read a review, he may have heard others speak about it—but whatever preceded this reader's experience of the first paragraph doesn't matter until suspense works its wonder. Nothing can keep the reader from reading on.

Synopsis

A synopsis is a much simplified condensation of the plot. It is designed to show the story's movement, beginning to end. Literary quality is seldom demonstrable in a synopsis. The reader of a synopsis can be attracted to an unusual character but cannot fall in love with characters as in a completed story. A synopsis can be effective as a plot summary by using short declarative sentences. The synopsis has to move fast from beginning to end because unlike the story itself, a summary does not duplicate the experience of reading.

T

Talking Shop with Other Writers

Most writers are not loners and will happily talk about writing craft with others. For nonfiction writers, exchanging ideas can be quite useful, but for fiction writers one caveat: Plot-driven writers have different mind-sets from character-driven writers, and advice or tips from one to the other can be hurtful unless you are fully aware of the differences. I shave every morning a writer who at times didn't armor himself against advice that discombobulated a good draft.

Telegraphing

Hinting or giving away clues or information about something to come later. Usually not a good idea unless it increases suspense. "Why was the door so difficult to keep closed?" signals the reader that the door is not locked. That's telegraphing.

Telephone Answering

What an odd item for a writer's help directory. Well, perhaps not. I know a few writers who need help in this field because they don't do a great job of scriptwriting when they are creating the message for callers to hear when the writer is not able or willing to answer because he can't interrupt writing his masterpiece or is just not there. My preferred short piece of writing for my telephone is "This machine takes messages for Sol Stein." It immediately tells the caller that they are talking to a machine. That's courteous. You have no idea how many people start out thinking a person is answering and say whom they want to speak to before they realize that the improperly written message is recorded.

Second, my message is brief, which is a second courtesy to a possibly busy person at the other end or anyone else who doesn't want to leave a message. Also the short message ties up the line minimally. And if I'm to get my writing done, I need to minimize my distractions.

Telling

In writing, the opposite of showing. Telling relates what happens in the scene, or offstage, or earlier, or elsewhere. A common flaw in fiction is to describe an offstage action. A narrator can tell a story, but in fiction a scene or a story is better seen by the reader rather than heard about. Telling takes a scene or action away from the reader's view and therefore diminishes the experience.

Tense

Most fiction is written in the past tense. A technique not frequently used in a work written in the past tense is for especially important scenes to shift into present tense as if the event pictured is happening in front of the reader's eyes. The change in tense can make a given scene more moving. For instance, "Francine was having a terrible time" is distancing the event from the reader. It can be brought closer by changing the tense to the present, as "Francine is having a terrible time." It's as if we are seeing the action rather than being told about it. "Francine is glancing right and left in the hope that someone might come" can be more effective than saying "Francine hoped someone would come." Note that I'm suggesting that you consider an *occasional* use of present tense when it would heighten the effect. I suspect the same story told entirely in present tense would seem artificial. It's easy enough to try its use sparingly and see how it might affect the reader's emotions.

Tension

I have noted elsewhere that writers of fiction are troublemakers. If they do their job well they give readers stress, strain, and pressure. Readers hate those things in life but enjoy them in fiction. The secret of causing tension is simple enough if you know that the word "tension" is derived from the Latin *tendere,* which means "to stretch." One of your characters is uncomfortable or worse. Don't make him comfortable. Stretch it out. Creating tension early in a story is valuable, especially if you can do it in the first three pages. What does not create tension is an explosion or finding a body in the first sentence or two of a novel. Tension needs to be prepared for, built up, preferably slowly. And the best way is to build tension through what a character sees and thinks. An example might be helpful:

The lawyer George Thomassy has appeared in several of my novels, beginning with *The Magician*. I keep revisiting him in other novels. In the opening of a novel called *The Touch of Treason* I tried to create tension in a vacant courtroom before a trial begins, even before the other participants arrive. It demonstrates how tension can be built even before the first scene begins. Here are the first paragraphs on page 1.

In the end you died. There could be a courtroom like this, Thomassy thought, all the good wood bleached white, the judge deaf to objections because He owned the place. The law was His, the advocacy system finished.

If that's what it was going to be like, George Thomassy wanted to live forever because here on earth, God willing or not, you could fight back.

Thomassy took in the grained thick wood of the raised perch, the bench from which the Honorable Walter Drewson would look down and judge defendant, defense counsel, prosecutor, witnesses, jury. Drewson would swivel in that now empty high-backed leather throne to see that his actors behaved according to the canons, protected from the players by a moat of flooring that no mortal crossed until he received the judge's sign. The others, kept at bay by the promise of contempt, sought comfort in the knowledge that the judge's vision was subject to the clouding of his contact lenses, and that under his severe black robe was hidden the ordinariness of a glen plaid suit and a spine that consisted of bones on a string.

At this point the reader has read only three paragraphs. There are a dozen more to come before the white-haired woman who is clerk of the court enters with "Good morning, Mr. Thomassy." What has been built by the stretching out is tension. The comfort of the reader is disturbed. This lawyer Thomassy seems not to be respectful of the prosecutor, the judge, or the court itself. Is Thomassy looking for trouble? Why? The reader needs relief of his curiosity. He has to know what is going to happen in that courtroom.

Tension is different from suspense. Suspense is building a strong desire in the reader to see what happens next. In these introductory paragraphs the reader has had no inkling of the plot. What has been built is a general tension about what will happen in that courtroom.

Theme

Both nonfiction and fiction have themes. A theme is an argument about subject matter, a thesis or concern. If you are writing nonfiction, your agent will ask you, "What is it about?" and mean not what facts are you presenting but what is your position about those facts. Similarly, if you're writing fiction, of course your characters are crucial but your agent will want to know what will make readers rush to a book by a novelist they haven't read before. Is it plot? Dubious, because if they know the plot they've taken some of the pleasure out of reading. Theme is often the author's view or vision of the subject matter, in fiction produced through characters.

I apologize for giving examples of themes from my own novels, but I know the themes relatively well, and for the works of some others I might be guessing. It is something of an embarrassment to take you backstage for a view of what the author thought his themes were. For instance, if anyone asked me what the working theme was of my debut novel, *The Husband*, I'd say it was about the hazards of divorce. What the publisher's people said on the jacket of the hardcover and on the paperback cover were all enticements for the reader, but were not the theme that enabled me to write the play and the book that was derived from it.

The subject matter of my next novel, *The Magician*, was the extortion rackets in high schools, but subject matter is not theme. The theme is the legerdemain of the law, how a terrific lawyer can make mincemeat of a just cause. Next came *Living Room,* my feminist novel. The flap copy says that the heroine was a public figure at twenty-eight, superbright, superbly attractive, a favorite of talk shows, recipient of the mayor's civic award, and yet she is about to kill herself for want of something beyond career success and the usual arrangements with a man. My theme for *Other People* was about one thing that divides the human race in two, rape, because the only men who view it with dread are sequestered in prison, while it has been reported that women of all ages fear rape from time to time. The theme is implicit in the story.

Time Away from a Draft

Most writers with discipline try to write for the same period at the same time each day. But as life will have it, emergencies happen to self, friends, and family that take the writer away from his scheduled work. The bright side of that bad news is that getting away from a book briefly can be a restorative. Work not from where you left off but from a few pages earlier or even a chapter earlier and see if the refreshment of time helps you improve your story.

Time to Write

The most frequent excuse is "I don't have enough time to write." A writer must make the time and defend it. Professionals will tell you to carve out a time of day for writing and stick to it. Your family, friends, and employers will attack. Defend yourself as if your life is at risk. Because it is if you are truly a writer—your work is a major part of your life, and nonwriters frequently don't understand that. Hang a sign on the doorknob of the room in which you write: **WRITER AT WORK—DO NOT DISTURB.**

Titles

A title has an important function. In a review or an ad or in a bookstore, the words in the title are the first thing a prospective reader will see unless you're famous. It's worth your time to come up with a good one. My late friend Ed McBain was a master craftsman in crime novels and had a hundred titles in print when he died. He knew something about his characters and plot beforehand but he insisted he would never begin the actual writing of a novel until he was satisfied with the title. He'd play with titles, even trying them in different font sizes, just to keep his reactions going. He'd keep all of them on display. He said that when he felt in danger of losing track of the story or the theme, he'd look at those pages of titles. It kept him focused.

Titles are important for arresting interest in both fiction and nonfiction. As a publisher I spent quite a bit of time helping with titles that weren't quite good enough. One hugeselling author used to come up with awful titles. I felt better about having to supply better titles when I learned that legendary Scribner's editor Maxwell Perkins received from a literary agent a manuscript with the title "O Lost." Someone at Scribner's succeeded in having the title changed to *Look Homeward, Angel*.

Titles attract agents, publishers, and book buyers. And it pays to give a good deal of attention to getting the best possible title. It will make a difference in the acceptance of the manuscript, and will sway chain buyers as well as individual browsers. The title of a book serves as an invitation to pick up, borrow, or buy. In addition to enticing the potential reader it must be appropriate for the audience that will be most receptive to the book.

How are titles selected? Usually by the author, sometimes with input from an agent or editor. As I write this, just yesterday I was giving a talk at a Rotary and the person who introduced me mentioned that she had recently scanned the manuscript of my memoir, which has had two titles. She mentioned both. The first title, *Passing for Normal,* got a big laugh from the audience, the second no audible reaction. Running a title before a group or at least several people *at the same time* is a way to get an early answer easily.

Keep in mind that perhaps your book will be published in Great Britain, and in other countries in translation. Fiction titles that sound good to great resonate differently in foreign languages. Try to avoid a title that doesn't translate well. I was careless in calling my second writing book *How to Grow a Novel.* That American expression doesn't translate well. In Germany, *How to Grow a Novel* became *Über das Schreiben.* Even in Britain, the publisher changed *Stein on Writing* to *Solutions for Writers,* and the second book became *Solutions for Novelists.* The upshot is that on the Web writers sometimes buy the same book under different titles.

I've just had a visit from an author of scientific nonfiction whose first book did well and who now has a better contract for a second book. He had a good working title that would attract people with a scientific interest in his subject. His subtitle, I pointed out, would arouse the curiosity of a much wider audience—he agreed—and all that was necessary was to reverse the two. Try it; it might work for you also.

Metaphors can make excellent titles for fiction, for example *The Heart Is a Lonely Hunter*. Narrative nonfiction titles should have some zing also. Other nonfiction should have titles that make it clear what the book is about and appeal to the most likely audience for the content.

It may be useful for the reader to eavesdrop on how the titles to my own books originated or evolved. The title of my first novel, *The Husband,* was derived from a play and is misleading. The play originally was performed at the Actors Studio under the title *Love or Marriage,* then bought for production in London. That title is meant to be enticing, but the two-letter key word "or" is easy to miss. Also, a popular song around at the time was "Love and Marriage." I later turned the play into a novel and sent it out under the noncontroversial but curiosity-invoking title *The Husband*.

The Magician as a title came quicker. The story is about a sixteen-year-old young man who performs magic tricks in high school, but the title also referenced a lawyer by the name of George Thomassy who has turned up in four of my novels and is a kind of magician in the courtroom. The book was selected by the Book of the Month Club, sold to 20th Century Fox, published in many languages, and, best of all, banned in a small city in Wisconsin along with F. Scott Fitzgerald's *The Great Gatsby* and *The Diary of Anne Frank*. It didn't take long for a million copies to be sold, so my advice is keep your title simple and get the book banned.

Ambiguity can sometimes make a good title. My next book was called *Living Room*. I worried a bit about the possible confusion with T. S. Eliot's play *The Living Room* but I liked the resonance of the title's meaning, room to live. It was an early feminist novel, which made the title even more suitable. Also it was short, familiar, and easy to remember.

An invented word that is easily understood can make a good title, as in *The Childkeeper.*

For *Other People,* my most complex novel to date, I kept the title as simple and ambiguous as possible. Meryl Streep wanted to play the leading part but the Hollywood mavens said she wasn't bankable.

The Resort is a simple title. The cover copy added, "Cliffhaven is a magnificent new resort near Big Sur in California, founded by a man with very special interest, catering to a very special clientele." The title *The Touch of Treason* came from Rebecca West, who said, "All men should have a touch of treason in their veins." On that same page I added an epigraph attributed to a character in several of my books, Archibald Widmer, who said, "The Soviets are chess players. We play checkers." The first publisher I sent the manuscript to—I was temporarily without an agent—asked me to dinner and before I sat down named a large sum I'd be embarrassed to mention here. The book has been twice optioned for the movies but, as usual, not produced. Some writers make a living from options to books that are perfectly suitable for the movies but are not made, often for reasons that are nonsensical.

A Deniable Man is probably an intriguing title for aficionados of espionage stories. That's the prime audience for that novel, hence an appropriate title.

The Best Revenge is of course from the saying "Living well is the best revenge." The publisher, in this case Random House, wanted a subtitle, "A Novel of Broadway," wherever the title appeared, on the front of the jacket, the title page, and so on. Of course the publisher's intention was to snag the readers with an interest in behind-the-scenes Broadway, but I would have preferred the ambiguity of *The Best Revenge*. If you skim the titles again, you'll see a common denominator. They are designed to have resonance and to intrigue.

Training

Observing generalities can get most people through life. Writers, however, have to learn to observe not only the easily observed but also the unobserved, including the minutiae that enable the reader to see what they're writing. The wink to a partner. The wandering gaze of a Lothario entering a room where a party is taking place. The rare and (she hopes) unobserved fidget of the woman wearing a new outfit that doesn't fit just right. The man who occasionally tugs at his too tight crotch. The man who thoughtlessly scratches the back of his neck from time to time for reasons unknown even to himself. The young child who gazes up at the giants in the room. Hemingway trained himself to see and hear the kind of significant minutiae that a painter might observe.

Treasure

Whatever your life has been up to this moment, you are host to a treasure box of experience that you may not have examined carefully. What was your single most embarrassing experience ever? Have you ever used that experience for one of your characters? What was your most triumphant moment?

Have you never had a triumphant moment? Whichever is true, jot down the essentials and try to use them in your writing.

What one person were you most excited to meet and why?

What opportunity did you miss? If the memory nags, try to invent something around the incident that you can use in a story.

What I'm suggesting is a construct of emotional moments in your own life that you can think about, manipulate, change, intensify, and use in the creation of a short story or novel, or that can clue you to a humanizing touch in narrative nonfiction.

Typeface Recommendation

I hope this isn't news to you, but nobody reads letters of the alphabet; they read whole words. A serif typeface is one that has curlicues. Those curlicues have an important function: They link the letters of a word, helping you read faster, not better. Don't hamper your agent or editor by using a sans serif type. That's the designation for the lean typefaces suitable for headlines, advertising captions, sometimes for very short copy under a photograph. Commercial advertisers sometimes use a sans serif type to squeeze more words into a small space but it does decrease readability somewhat. I use the most common serif type, 12-point Times Roman, which is in wide usage. You want the reader to be involved in the content, not in the style of the words.

U

Uncertainty When Beginning Fiction

Before starting on the journey of a first draft, you should have visualized the protagonist and antagonist at least in generalities, what their conflict is, and one or more places where the story might take place. The first scene needs to snare the reader's attention, but you may not know what the first scene will be just yet. That shouldn't keep you from imagining a place you know well, say your own home, and then perhaps deciding that that location is unsuitable but X would be better. It's a way of self-stimulation, turning a wrong choice into a right choice you hadn't previously imagined! You may not know yet where the story is going. Not to worry. If you're writing a western and imagining a crowded subway car, you will quickly find a more suitable environment to put your characters in. What I am suggesting is that the places of a story can come to you in dreams or in self-trickery in which you throw away a ridiculous choice. The occasional beginner, who hasn't thought much about his story and hasn't learned this trick of the ridiculous, can try another method. Open a dictionary or thesaurus at random and go fishing for words that will clue your imagination to specific images. Or phone a friend and ask him to name the oddest places he's ever been to. His memory can jump-start yours. If you can jump-start an automobile, be advised that jump-starting your imagination is equally useful in an emergency!

Usage

In writing "usage" usually refers to how a word or phrase is commonly used. Rigid use of grammar in speech can make a good character stuffy. Usage becomes more colloquial among young people, who use neologisms of their own invention. Usage within an occupation or sport is often unfamiliar to outsiders and prohibits communication until such time as the usage spreads.

V

Verbs

English is a great language for writers in part because it consists of two streams, the Anglo-Saxon active verbs and the multisyllabic words of French or Latin origin. Active verbs strengthen sentences. Passive verbs weaken sentences. "Thomassy tore up the summons" is strong. "The summons was torn up by Thomassy" is weaker. Choose among active verbs carefully. Warning: "Thomassy crumpled the summons" is weaker than "Thomassy tore up the summons," but may be more accurate. Accuracy, clarity, and strength are the objectives, but the music of a sentence has to be taken into account. The best of our writers take the time to ferret out of their memory (or a thesaurus) the precise words that are both accurate and strong.

Verisimilitude

It means seeming to be true or real, lifelike. Edith Wharton called verisimilitude "the truth of art." She shook a gloved finger at "the slovenly habit of some novelists of tumbling in and out of their characters' minds, and then suddenly drawing back to scrutinize them from the outside as the avowed Showman holding his puppets' strings." Her comment reminds me of when in my youth I performed magic tricks and was asked so many times, "How did you do that?" Of course if I told how it would take the pleasure out of the game. Wharton is cussing out writers who inject themselves or anything else that disturbs the reader's sense of being *in the story*.

Villains

To make fiction credible, villains should be thought of as opponents. Their actions and purpose need to be credible—from their point of view. Villains need to be effective in clashes with protagonists. Their motives ought to seem sensible from their perspective. Attractive villains are more compelling than those who are immediately distasteful in what they say or do. The sneering entirely bad villain of yesteryear challenges credibility in all forms of writing.

Visualization

With the advent of movies in the early twentieth century and the addition of television in midcentury, visual storytelling had a profound effect on readers who got used to being moved by what they saw rather than by what they were told. As a result, effective writing became more visual than it had been in the past. I have sometimes suggested to writers that they go through a draft, marking a *V* in a corner of each page that is visually satisfying. The temptation of writers is to relate what happened in a scene rather than showing it happening. See also **Show, Don't Tell** and **Backstory**.

Visualization, detail, and quotation made it seem as if the writer had been a witness, privy to public and private happenings, as in Tom Wolfe's *The Right Stuff* and Norman Mailer's *The Executioner's Song*. The authors themselves would sometime appear as characters in the new nonfiction. Complex and disordered events were made highly readable by writers who used real events to create stories that seemed true. And were. The success of the new forms drew verbal praise from person to person and landed books on bestseller lists, providing strength and notoriety to the new nonfiction. The techniques of narrative storytelling began to take their place in magazines and newspapers. Features and multipart series presented readers with factual material in forms that were a pleasure to read. Stories based on truth and events that really happened were welcomed by readers who had avoided the dry nonfiction of yesteryear. The reader's acceptance of narratives hinged on the belief that they were true. The few writers who cheated and filled the new form with inventions were publicly decried, and provided the rest of us with a useful wariness.

It took centuries to develop the form of the contemporary novel, which keeps evolving. The new forms of nonfiction also evolve, combining information with the fascination of stories, a high standard in their re-creation of life. By whatever names the new nonfiction is called, it is part of a single movement, with emphasis on characters, protagonists and villains, in an environment of gradually released information about people and events in the perilous joyride of life.

W

Weekends

This subject deserves special attention from writers early in their careers. Most people in most occupations work during the week from Monday through Friday and consider weekends their own or family time. But not writers of books. Nonfiction writers are better off than novelists because nonfiction can be organized into manageable sections and each can be dealt with separately as time allows. Novelists have a tougher task; it may take years to complete a first draft—and then there are the drafts that come afterward. And novel writing when taken seriously is a haunting occupation. The writer is haunted by his characters and his themes, and by scenes to come and scenes that didn't work as well as he would have liked. It's a long journey that possesses the writer, provides occasional joy when things go right, but also can be like a wound that takes its own time to heal. Writing novels can't follow the norm of weekends off from work. Saturday and Sunday are simply other days, not holidays. As the book grows, working on it can become compulsive. Ask any family member of a novelist as the novel—a new member of the family—takes over and begins to claim priorities.

You may be able to work out a routine that is less obtrusive to family life and provides weekends away from work. I envy you.

What the Reader Wants

In fiction, the reader wants an experience different from and greater than his or her everyday experiences in life. This doesn't mean a car crash or a lot of violence. The utter frustration and difficulty of trying to thread a needle can be a moving experience for a reader witnessing it. If the woman doing the threading is in a rush to sew a button on in order to wear a particular piece of clothing, that tension can increase the experience. If the needle is an old one with a very narrow opening for thread, the task becomes harder and annoying. If she needs to be somewhere else at a given time, again the tension of threading a needle increases. The trouble with this example, as you will already have noticed, is that needle threading is so ordinary a task. But if her eyesight is not what it used to be and the necessity of being somewhere in time is today especially important . . . you get the idea: Mountains can be made out of needle threading. The art will be in how her anxiety is depicted. To say the woman seems nervous is telling. If she tries to bite the thread and fails . . . if she drops the needle in the thick carpet and has to get down on her hands and knees to find it . . . you get the point. Show, don't tell.

In nonfiction, the reader wants information presented in a visual or tactile way. Frequently, humans are involved. Items, minute or gigantic, can be seen and, if appropriate, felt through the words by which the item is displayed, manipulated, lost, or found. When one says that nonfiction is "coming alive," it means that the reader is getting information by seeing a process as it is described or observed.

What to Write?

In writing fiction, are you writing the kind of story that you enjoyed reading before you turned to writing? If you're writing nonfiction, are you dealing with subject matter that interested you in other people's books? If you're writing narrative nonfiction, have you digested the guidelines for fiction and nonfiction because both will come into play in narrative nonfiction? I'm told that among journalists, narrative fiction calls for a feature-writing sensibility.

What Your Book Is About (Fiction and Nonfiction)

It is true that when starting out on a novel, you're supposed to be thinking about your principal character and his and her needs and wants and, yes, character. But that character doesn't live in a vacuum; he or she is in need, wants something, is blocked, and you are off thinking about *story*. If you do that, you will not only be helping yourself write the story, you will be helping your future agent because the agent, when testing a publisher's interest in seeing your manuscript, will have to say first *what the book is about,* and that's your story. And don't get highfalutin and say your story is about the nature of man or something similar. It may well be, but it won't help your agent place the book. For example, if I were to say what my novel *The Magician* is about, I wouldn't say justice—that's too abstract. I would say it's about extortion rackets in high schools and two sixteen-year-olds clashing over the refusal of the protagonist to pay dues to the gang leader for the use of his own locker. That is specific enough to stimulate a response. So it's a good idea to come up with one sentence that describes your story by provoking the listener into wanting to hear more. Besides, it will be a useful sentence for the salesmen who have to interest all the booksellers in their territory. The point is to be specific but not so specific as to need a second sentence. It's not a bad idea to memorize that sentence and also to keep it in large letters on a three-by-five-inch card in full view as you write the book. Yes, if your imagination strays from that story and if the new story sounds better, tear up the three-by-five card and write a new one!

Of course if your book is nonfiction, you will need to do something similar, that is, come up with a sentence that shows your take on the subject to be different, appealing, and possibly exciting.

When Is a Manuscript Ready to Be Sent to an Agent or a Publisher?

When you are relatively certain that you cannot improve it any more, it is in the right professional format, and you have checked it against the instructions and criteria in this book. Most reputable agents do not do rewriting, though they sometimes make useful suggestions to clients whose work looks like it may be salable when finished. (That means it's not ready for submission.) The writer cannot judge whether a manuscript is ready shortly after finishing the last page. An experienced writer will give a manuscript a rest, at least a week and preferably longer, to be better able to judge his own work. Friends and relatives are of little help unless they are also experienced writers, because the opinions of laymen about a work in progress are seldom of value. An agent's opinion is more valuable because the agent has to sell the book to a publisher, and if the book is not ready, it is the agent's reputation as well as the author's that will be at risk. Writing either fiction or nonfiction is a profession. Individuals trained in other professions need to know that writing an article, story, or book requires a lot of specific knowledge not available in a normal curriculum. Writing well requires experience and the study of some existing books, perhaps including this one.

When to Write
There are lots of legends about writing time. John le Carré tried to stick to a specified time of day as if he were employed in a business of his own creation. Gore Vidal was fussy about starting to work, but once started, he found it difficult to stop. Chekhov insisted that writers should work every day. James Baldwin did his best work very late at night when the world around him was sleeping. That might have been inspired by the fact that he was the oldest of nine children and began writing stories when the others were asleep.

Where to Start If You're Writing Fiction
Begin with something that moves you or did move you a great deal some time ago. Think about it. Make some undisciplined notes about it, whatever comes to mind when you think about what moves or moved you.

Where to Write
A jail cell is not recommended. Intrusive noises and arguments slip through the barriers. What the writer needs is a

cliché: a place that is reasonably comfortable to work in and where he will not be interrupted. Privacy is not private if the writer's brain is subject to interruption. A serious writer needs uninterrupted isolation from the rest of the world, especially its sounds and people.

Why Readers Read Fiction

To experience some of the pleasures of life vicariously, to experience danger without the threat of real harm, to know what it is like to be other people in other circumstances, to travel without the need of any transportation but the pages of a magazine or book at little risk of anything but time.

Why Write?

It is a means of offering what you think you know to others. In the words of Atul Gawande, it's a declaration of membership in a community and a willingness to contribute to it. Gawande's book *Better* is a masterly book about medical doctoring that has a lot to say that's applicable to a thinking writer.

Working Habits

At the end of my writing day, I leave a short note to myself about what I plan to do the next morning. It saves time. When I'm allegedly not working, ideas still pop into my head about the book I'm working on. These notes are helpful to me and a nuisance to the person who helps me find them if I don't stow them in the designated place I use for notes. Belatedly I received a gift of two blank notebooks with lined pages, one labeled "Sol's Memory Book" and the other "Sol's Upstairs Memory Book," for my bedside night table. I've learned to use them instead of scraps of paper, and the people in my life have been nicer to me since.

Working Hours

I've worked with many writers over the years whose work hours are not similar to the usual eight hours a day, five days a week. Journalists for newspapers may work more "normal" hours than most novelists. One important writer I worked with in the early years seemed to do much if not most of his writing after midnight, when interruptions were unlikely. He also lit each cigarette with the butt end of the previous cigarette, and oftentimes a small glass of Scotch was not too far away. My advice is to find the time of day in which you are likely to be able to work often and allow it to become as habit-forming as sleep.

Writerly

Not a word that is adequately defined—or defined at all—in most dictionaries or thesauruses. It means "well written," and is the opposite of "consciously literary." "Consciously literary" is amateurish writing attempting to sound literary but actually sounding like a beginner's fumbling with precious phrases. I use "writerly" to mean "with expertise in the precise and fresh use of words and images." It is a compliment. Writerly writing makes use of similes, metaphors, and visual detail. It is not enough to eliminate clichés, expressions that are familiar because they have been used many times before. A *creative* writer won't say, "Clothes don't make the man," a cliché, but he might freshen the idea with "The important creases are in the brain, not in the pants." Another example I've used is actually taken from life. When in the middle of a neighboring town I stepped on a large wad of gum someone had discarded on the sidewalk, and I was trying unsuccessfully to get it off my shoe. This was in front of a barbershop, and a barber I will always be grateful to came out of the shop and handed me some paper towels so I could go on my way. There's a cliché for that kind of happening: "The more you try to get rid of it, the worse it seems to get."

The intent to praise is often drowned in a cliché. Senator Daniel Patrick Moynihan, one of the few eggheads in national office, wanted to say something superlative about a man I knew well. In the *Congressional Record* Moynihan said: "I think it is safe to say Leo Cherne's life helped to redeem the 20th century." Now that's writerly.

Writer's Block
Warning: This suggestion is not for young children, the excessively timid, or people on life support. The easiest solution for writer's block is to open a good dictionary to any page and read slowly just the words, not the definitions, one at a time. If two pages of words don't stimulate a single thought that might just ignite your imagination, take up bookkeeping. P.S. Some writers get over their block by writing fast, I mean really fast, faster than they've ever written before, as if a hungry wolf were chasing them.

Writer's Courage

Some of the best writing about writing has emphasized the writer's need for courage. Joyce Carol Oates, who teaches writers at Princeton and is herself a prolific and courageous writer, has said, "Any form of art is a species of exploration and transgression. To write is to invade another's space." The writer is butting into the reader's mind, not with conventional things but with what is new and forceful. Think Kafka, Melville, Hemingway, if you like—they don't take the world as it is; they punch their news to the reader. Writing is not an occupation for the timid, the neat, the predictable. People who write can be as nice or mean as they were brought up to be, but in the act of writing they have to say what other people only think.

Writing About Faces

Most of us rush through busy lives using two main categories of faces, people we don't know, and people we recognize from having seen them before and perhaps knowing them a little.

For the faces of humans we writers often rely on rough categories: a scowling face, an insipid look, a soft face, a hard face. In writing, with a little work we can provide a face with individuality, as in: "Sam's habit when anyone was talking to him was to let his eyes roll upward as if the sky and not a human were speaking to him." Journalists reporting how a person looks might be on the lookout for what is special, individual, charming, or annoying in a real person's manner, looks, expressions, or voice. In fiction, give any character that has a speaking part a real face. Be careful not to overload a face with detail—one special characteristic will do.

Writing as an Obsession

There are people who say that writing is an obsession. There are also people who say studying many years to be a physician is an obsession. The conundrum is that no one seems to say that becoming an engineer is an obsession. Are we talking sense? What seems to be true is that a high interest in the arts as a young person may lead to a life of poor monetary reward. That is certainly a possibility, but learning to write well is useful in many avenues of life, even business, where the use of language can be a disaster or an advantage. It is said that those who would long to be a writer are infatuated, besotted, smitten with words and what they might create. Lorrie Moore famously said, "First try to be something, anything else. You should become a writer only if you have no choice. Writing has to be an obsession—it's only for those who say, 'I'm not going to do anything else.'" I think that's nonsense, which is a polite way of saying what I really think. Writing is a choice of a way of spending a working life that lets you off the hook if you decide you don't like it or haven't sufficient talent in the use of words to be productive as a writer. But if you take to it, the writing life can be gloriously rewarding even if you're struggling with perfecting a potentially important or useful work of nonfiction or, heaven forbid, a novel! A writer must read a lot of other people's writing. A writer must think. A writer must organize the nuances of words and the intricacies of language in a way that will move or delight readers. It's a great and valuable occupation that challenges and extends the life of your brain; a novel that's done to your absolute satisfaction will continue to bring you joy for the rest of your life.

Writing as a Profession

Fiction and nonfiction writing both require dedication, a willingness to study a wide range of published writers, and an ability to draft and redraft and revise the same material many times. If fiction is your métier, in a world that is racing by, you need to develop a habit of observation, noting the minutiae as well as the conspicuous and grand, the color of dry sand and the color of wet sand. How does a person look when he is momentarily lost?

The garrulous should know that writing even articles and short stories, much less books, is lonely and at times arduous. In beginning years especially the postman becomes an important figure in your daily life. If you write books, though books may be sold five or seven days a week, royalties earned above the advance are paid twice a year. One of the hardest questions to answer is "What is your annual income?" Don't talk money to a real writer. He writes because he wants to and has to. Some writers make a comfortable living from their work if they learn to husband advances for dry periods.

Writing is a highly competitive occupation in that the activity when learned and done well is so rewarding to the ambitious imagination that at any one time a lot of writers are competing for the same space or reward. The occupation, while held in high esteem by educated others, is usually lonely. Journalists may work in dangerous locations away from home and family, sometimes for long periods of time.

For many writers, a weekend day is almost the same as a weekday because it is hard to skip a day or two of work and get back to it on Monday. On any day you may think you have finished work, but ideas relating to your work pop up, and you'd better record each idea in a few words or you'll find it hard to remember when Monday comes around. It has been said that you are open for incoming business all the time. To the beach you take a beach towel but also a pen and paper. You interrupt yourself—and others—if words come to you out of the blue. When at work, a carpenter can put his hammer aside for the interruption and then get back to work. In writing, interruptions can disrupt family relations and make you forget a wonderful phrase you'd just thought of but hadn't yet written. Then again, Disraeli wrote novels and ended up as prime minister.

Remembering names of people and places is a difficult skill as one gets beyond three-quarters of a century in age. There are substitutes: Slim, portable notebooks that can slip into a breast pocket. Post-its to mark places in a book or in a newspaper that needs to have an article clipped. More than one pen because pens sometimes, though rarely, run out of ink, and you may be left helpless to scribble a reminder of something that is just right for your next story.

I have never heard of a professional writer retiring at sixty-five. Or seventy. Or seventy-five. That says something, doesn't it?

Writing Workshops

I have attended many types of workshops and classes over the course of a long life. In a good many of them the writing students read their stories or part of them aloud. Some students are good actors and read bad stories well, using their voice to cover up inadequate writing. Also I've observed young writers of considerable talent who don't read aloud well because of a fear of acting in public, or of thin voices they cannot help. The teacher or leader of the class sometimes sits by until the end. The problem is that the leader is in the same boat as the others; he cannot trim away the successful or unsuccessful recital from the words. That's why I began my Chapter One seminars for students who took my courses at the University of California at Irvine, which proved to be the most successful teaching experience I have had (and students continue to tell me the same for them). Here's how it worked. We met once a week around a very long table, or two long tables together. After they'd had some instruction, each week three students were designated to be "on deck" for the following week. They were to bring in their stories or, more often, the first chapter of their novels-in-progress in as many copies as there were students plus one for me. When these were distributed, all of us except the writer were reading that first chapter at the same time, marking things with a pen as if we were all editors.

The results were amazing because even beginning writers are experienced readers and can pick up errors other people make quicker than they can their own. The results were discussed. If someone's suggested excision or change was wrong,

I discussed the fault and how to remedy it. This worked so well that we attracted to the seminar writers who'd had books published (one had more than thirty!), so the seminars then contained experienced nonfiction writers and journalists eager to learn fiction. Writers were learning from each other's mistakes—and how to fix faults—much faster than is possible in a class in which writers pretend to be actors and read their scripts aloud.

The Distinguished Instructor Award I received from the university in competition with some five hundred others was really for the concept of this method of teaching, which I commend to other groups of writers and their instructors.

Y

You

Are not any of the characters if you are writing fiction. I know, you've lived through something or other and would like to use it. Fine. But give your character traits that are the opposite of yours and you will be much better able to manipulate him or her as you make your fiction interesting. John Mortimer, creator of *Rumpole of the Bailey,* had a fine conversion trick he admitted to his biographer. His character Rumpole provided a sly way of carrying the writer's own views on law and politics. Mortimer was justly concerned that Rumpole might sound "rather leftish and off-putting," Mortimer's characterization of himself, and so he made Rumpole crusty, conservative, and, in his words, "much more appealing."

This trick of opposites can be useful in other ways to camouflage the fact that a base character is modeled on someone the author knows and despises in real life. Once, when editing the work of a rather famous writer, I discovered not only that a thoroughly detestable character in his book was modeled after someone he loathed in life, but that he used the same name. How was an editor to know that? When the author's book came out, I was present at a book promotion event when the man in question came over and introduced himself with his real name, knowing what a shock it would be. Fortunately, he was not in a mood to sue and took the affront lightly.

If you're underweight, try an overweight character's point of view. Don't turn it into propaganda, but get inside the character. Tie a big pillow around your waist and walk around your home. If that doesn't give you a character, keep the pillow on and walk around your neighborhood and you'll find yourself thinking inside a character's head.

Your Assets as Liabilities in Character Creation

In creating characters, we sometimes use our own characteristics, usually favorably because we'd like to be like that. For creating characters, it's sometimes useful to look at the opposite of how you see yourself. For instance, suppose you are tall. Did you ever walk around a submarine and feel the ceilings were too low? I was once a guest in a New Jersey house built by Hessian mercenaries at the time of the American Revolution. The Hessians must have been quite a bit shorter than I am because in hurrying downstairs I hit my head hard on the lintel of the too-short door. My alleged asset, height, was a liability in that house. I found that useful in characterization, the positive and negative values of height. Any other characteristics can be changed to their opposite, good to bad, bad to good. Use your own assets or liabilities first if you can, and if you find that somewhat uncomfortable you're on the right track.

PART 2: PUBLISHING

A

Acquiring Editors

The title may have once designated an editor with authority to buy a book, but even in the good days of yesteryear an editor would usually consult with colleagues and the publisher prior to any significant purchase commitment. In large companies with editorial boards, an editor's proposal to purchase a manuscript calls for a presentation at the editorial board or a similar meeting with financial projections and other information for groupthink. Once upon a time instinct, taste, and experience governed a decision to buy a book. Publishing companies that have become corporations with multiple publishing units attempt to convert the acquisition process into a system that is supposedly influenced more by numbers than by experience. In heaven, the great publishers and editors of the early twentieth century look down at the procedure and sometimes laugh or cry.

Once a book is assigned to an editor, in the publishing organization it becomes "his" or "her" book. The editor's identification with a book is strong within the organization and in the editor's psyche as well during the publication process and beyond.

Advance or Royalty Advance (Payment Received from a Publisher)

The guaranteed amount paid by the publisher to the author through his agent against future earned royalties for copies sold as well as the author's percentage of subsidiary rights. This payment is normally made in steps, part on signature, part on successful completion of the manuscript, part on publication. The author or his agent will receive royalty reports, usually semiannually. If a book ceases to generate income, any part of the advance that is not recouped is spoken of as "an unearned advance." An advance is "earned out" when the sales of books and subsidiary rights have earned the amount of the advance, and future sales will earn royalties above the advance for the author.

Agents

A book agent is the person who represents the author's work and solicits editors who might be interested in publishing it. Unlike most authors, agents are in contact with many editors and know each editor's preferences and methods of work. Some agents also solicit foreign publications and publishers, usually through subagents who work in the foreign territory. Contract negotiation and review are also important tasks of an agent. Agents review royalty reports and receipts. An agent will also serve as a buffer between author and editor in the event of disagreement.

A few agents play an important role in the revision of drafts. Prestigious agents can sometimes get bigger advances for their writers. Most agents are good at getting better terms than an author might get on his own. A writer without an agent is in a plane without a pilot. To take off, use an experienced agent.

Nothing pleases an agent more than discovering a previously unpublished writer of high talent with a finished manuscript. Newcomers sometimes ask why they need an agent. Professional writers know the answer. An agent has much easier access to the process of manuscript consideration. An agent can forestall submissions that are not ready to be seen by acquiring editors. Moreover, an experienced agent knows the preferences of different editors and publishers, and submissions of his writers will be read much sooner than an unknown's manuscript that lands in the slush pile and is probably looked at first by a relatively new editor or an entry-level assistant. Also, an agent may have previously negotiated a change in or the omission of an undesirable clause in a publisher's standard contract, and another writer might benefit from that precedent.

In the best of circumstances, the writer and agent bond. The agent may suggest remedies for weaknesses that should be fixed before a manuscript is submitted. An agent can highlight strengths with far more credibility than an author can. Submitting a manuscript by a new author can involve a lot of work that often exceeds the commission received. Moreover, an experienced agent will superintend payments beyond the advance if such money is forthcoming. The first thing an author should look for in an agent is experience with the type of book he has written. The second is a feeling of comfort with the person. "Loving" a book is a valuable attribute, but understanding a book is at least as important for making the sale. To agents as well as editors nothing is as thrilling as the discovery of new talent.

B

Backlist
Books published in prior seasons that continue to sell and are still listed in the publisher's catalog. When friends die one feels pain. When books die, few take notice. The accounting departments of publishers set certain minimum levels for life support of a backlist book. Backlist books that no longer sell are remaindered (see **Remainders**). New publishers might profitably help support their efforts by delving into neglected backlist books, acquiring them from the original publisher, and giving them another life. Where would Shakespeare's dramas be without revivals?

Jason Epstein's excellent book, *Book Business: Publishing Past, Present, and Future,* is very clear about the importance of backlists. He reports that when Random House was owned by its two founders, a slow season didn't matter much because "next year or the year after would be better. Meanwhile the backlist kept the company afloat."

Biggest Changes in Publishing as a Business
In the early part of the twentieth century, book-publishing firms were run mainly by their founders, who were "book

people," individuals whose main interest in many cases was not in commerce but in books and their contents. Of course they tried, often successfully, to make enough of a profit from year to year to keep them happy. If one had a huge bestseller, as we did from time to time at Stein and Day, the year's profits zoomed, and inevitably the following year's profits were down if there was no blockbuster on the list. We knew this cycle well. When Wall Street and bean counters took over publishing managements, the ups and downs frustrated the financial people, who didn't understand the business well enough to know that blockbusters come occasionally and don't increase in quantity year by year.

Book publishing is unlike other businesses in that financial success depends on finding new "products," books that people will want to buy. Books are not coffeemakers or similar objects that can be manufactured at will. The industry depends on what writers have in their heads and are putting down on paper. The culturally most valuable books are sometimes the least reliable reproducers.

The sale of books transmitted electronically to handheld platforms, or downloaded to computers, usually at a much lower cost than the hardcover book, is a historically important development.

The culture of publishing in the twentieth century was transformed by mergers, foreign ownership, and a new kind of emphasis on the bottom line in an industry that needs to find, edit, and produce thousands of different products each year. For more detailed information about the huge changes

I recommend *Book Business: Publishing Past, Present, and Future* by Jason Epstein.

Book Advertising

I can't count the number of times in my career in publishing that I heard authors complain about a lack of advertising because they thought of advertising as the way any product could be sold. The truth is that a tiny percentage of published trade books, fiction or nonfiction, receives any advertising at all. In some cases advertising is designed to meet a contractual agreement or to pacify a bestselling author. Space advertising is expensive in relation to other means of publicizing new books, except, possibly, for new novels by writers with a large following. Nonfiction books about high-profile current political or other issues often enjoy an early sale as a result of a huge announcement ad that starts the crowd moving, but a newsbreak about something important in the book may start the ball rolling at much less expense.

Nonfiction that is of practical value to people in a certain trade deserves small space informative ads in magazines catering to people in that trade. However, getting a review in such publications can be even more effective. Some people will read a review with excitement if the book seems of practical value *but don't think of buying it*. If the publisher knows about the review ahead of time, a small space "reminder" ad in the same issue can be worthwhile. In academic circles the first reaction may be to ask their library to obtain a copy. A small space ad can sometimes make a difference if it raises a practical reason for prolonged ownership.

Book Banning

I am not objective about this subject for two reasons. I deplore book banning by librarians or library administrators. It occurs from time to time but is almost always reversed in due course. My second novel, *The Magician,* was banned in a small Midwestern city back in 1971 along with F. Scott Fitzgerald's *The Great Gatsby* and *The Diary of Anne Frank.* I learned that once the banning was publicized, people especially in Wisconsin were driving up to three hundred miles to find copies of my banned book, which in time sold more than a million copies, helped by its selection by the Book of the Month Club and my appearance on the Johnny Carson television show, but most especially because of the news stories about the banning. If you are a creative writer, your creativity might include a scheme for getting your book banned, too. The American Library Association publishes a list of books that have been banned in the United States.

Book Clubs

For half a century beginning in 1926 when the Book of the Month Club was started, clubs were a means for people living in areas without bookstores to find out what was newly available. It was the convenience of getting books by mail and at some reduction in price that seemed to count most to members, but in specialized clubs, for example the Military Book Club or the Science Fiction Book Club, a kind of community of interest also mattered. Even higher-browed book clubs thrived for a while. A book's being selected by a club fortifies favorable reviews. It also serves to advise the public of the availability of the selected book. Amazon rang a change by offering most new books at a discount. Also it is now easy to obtain used books by mail, usually from secondhand dealers and stores. I organized a highbrow book club called the Mid-Century Book Society. The judges were W. H. Auden, Jacques Barzun, and Lionel Trilling. The first ad was a double-truck (two adjacent pages) in *The New York Times Book Review* that depicted a table around which these three gentlemen sat waiting for you the reader to fill the fourth chair. The response was nearly sensational considering that the offering was only one book of poems. The club survived for years largely because it published an excellent monthly magazine, which was sent only to members who bought at least four books a year.

Book Clubs for Reading Groups

As the era of big book clubs became a smaller factor in publishing, book groups of readers began to flourish in the United States. Many were of female readers who would meet, usually in the home of one of the members, perhaps once a month with all of the participants having read the same book announced at a previous meeting, almost always a novel. Publishers cooperated in providing a list of questions that might stimulate discussion among the book club members.

Book Manufacturing

Some manufacturing methods make life difficult for the reader. The physical part of reading a book should be a pleasure. Somewhere along the line carelessness set in; the binding of some books is so bad that the reader has to use force to keep the book open. Moreover, forcible attempts to break the spine enough to be able to read and turn pages make the book when finished—if finished—a shame on a shelf next to properly manufactured books, which can be opened to any page and held there without force. This bookmaking disaster has been visited also on paperbacks that have the same flaw—they're hard to keep open.

Bookselling

I have singled out one bookseller of the many who during the early part of the twentieth century owned a store that sold only books, who loved and cared for his beloved merchandise, and in this instance became a major figure in America's second city, Chicago, a prince in a hierarchy that had no king. His name was Stuart Brent and he wrote a book about bookselling that he called *The Seven Stairs,* because that's how many you had to climb to get to his store before it became a street-level emporium and Brent became a magnet for the art-loving cognoscenti of Chicago, which happens to be the Middle American city where I was born. On tour for a new book there were several requisites, like doing the important Chicago TV interview show of Irv Kupcinet, which no touring actor or author would turn down, and paying a visit, however quick, to Stuart Brent's book emporium. I recall once coming into his store after spending some moments looking at the books displayed in the large streetfront window. It was a time when Jacqueline Susann was the rage across the country and number 1 on the charts. I went inside and after embracing Stuart I said, "I didn't see Jackie Susann's in the window."

"Hey," he responded, "I sell *books!*"

His display window was full of the books Stuart thought Chicago ought to be reading! And Chicago loved him in turn. He had his own fictitious book club, meaning the list of book-loving Chicagoans whom he'd advise the moment he had stock of a new and worthwhile book. Stuart Brent was prescient. Chapter 1 of *The Seven Stairs* starts out:

> I might as well tell you what this book is about. Years ago I started to write a memoir about a young fellow who wanted to be a book dealer and how he made out. I tore it up when I discovered the subject had already been covered by a humorist named Will Cuppy in a book called How to Become Extinct.

There are still some booksellers like him all over the country, and in Canada and Europe, too, who are hanging in to a bookselling trade that is struggling to compete in the electronic New World.

Bookselling on Consignment

A practice established during the Great Depression in the early 1930s was for publishers to sell books to bookstores with the right to return them for full credit if unsold. Publishers took the risk, since it was presumed that their sales estimates were better than the booksellers' sales estimates. That is not necessarily true, but it was the accepted custom at the time to sell the books on consignment—in effect, to lend the books to the bookstores to see if they would sell.

Alfred Knopf's comment on this strange custom was "Gone today, here tomorrow." If booksellers underestimate significantly the demand for a book and the book jumps onto the bestseller list, they can often restock quickly from a wholesaler to avoid lost sales.

Book Tours

I don't regret missing the time when authors were sent on book tours. I did that several times, once doing twenty-one cities in twenty days. Given the contemporary crush at airports, the frequency of delayed flights, missed connections, security issues, and so on, it would be heroic and impossible. In those bad old days, I once had to get from Tucson, Arizona, to Dallas for an early-morning broadcast interview, with a few hours in between for sleep. The plane's takeoff was aborted because of a mechanical problem that could not be resolved quickly, and it was the last plane heading for Dallas that night. With great good luck I was sitting next to a man with clout who was able to reach the airline's senior management, as a result of which a plane coming into Phoenix was ordered to drop off its full planeload and instead of retiring for the night, fly on to Dallas with three passengers; the young man who had an early-morning TV interview, the man with pull, and his companion. The only unhappy people aboard were the crew, who had expected to rest in Phoenix for the night. As the plane descended to the Dallas airport, the senior flight attendant got on the speaker and said, "We hope you've had a nice trip. Thank you for flying Eastern," which was not the airline we were on!

In those days, when a flight was landing late, an author could ask the crew to notify the airline that an author was aboard and was due on station so-and-so for an announced interview at a certain time. On arrival, there'd be a motorized cart ready to take the author quickly to a waiting taxi, all arranged by the courteous airline. Try that now and what you'll hear is "Tough!"

The upshot is that touring was extremely tiring. In some places the interviews were disappointing, and in larger cities you'd be asked to do a radio show, a TV show, and perhaps a newspaper interview, with no union to protect you from overtime. Now a "tour" can be done in one studio and passed out to a dozen stations in other cities.

Bound Galleys

These are bound to simulate a paperback, distributed by the publisher a good many weeks before the official release date. The covers tend to be plain, that is without artwork, and the uncorrected galleys are so labeled. These are distributed to booksellers at conventions and by sales reps who are armed with them when they visit important retail accounts and chains. The purpose, of course, is to get orders for the book in advance. First-time authors should be aware of this process and be sure to see a bound galley and inform the editor if there are any serious mistakes or significant absences. Also check dedications and other front matter. Once corrections are made, the book is in final form and will be manufactured in quantity. Warning: Watch out for anything amiss in the body of the book. I once received galleys in which fourteen sections of a novel had been put entirely in italics. I was stunned because it changed the book drastically. A phone call remedied it but the mistake might have slipped by because I was three thousand miles from home base when I received the galleys.

Byline

The author's name or pseudonym on a manuscript.

C

Categories of Fiction

Mysteries, crime novels, thrillers, and suspense novels all come under the heading of "commercial fiction," which is somewhat of a misnomer because the writers and publishers of all kinds of fiction are hopeful that their books will sell. Another name for these books is "popular fiction," but some higher-browed fiction can be quite popular. "Women's fiction" as a term is unfair to women. "Romance fiction" is a pseudonym for lowbrow love fiction. "Children's books" are for children but age levels are important. "Young adult" as a category has a pejorative ring to me because in my family I was offered only adult fiction when I was young. In reality, if one has to categorize, there are two main kinds of fiction. Commercial fiction is usually written by writers whose main intent is focused on getting paid for the work, and the stories themselves are plot-driven. Literary fiction aims higher, lasts longer if done well, and may or may not provide long sustenance for the writer. Much literary fiction is character-driven, which means you remember Sherlock Holmes and Dr. Watson, but not necessarily the details of their escapades.

Chain Stores

In the early twentieth century traditional bookstores were located in most big cities and in smaller towns with book-reading populations. These stores usually had owners and clerks who worked there because they were "book people"; they loved books as cultural rather than material objects, liked getting to know their customers' tastes, and were able to recommend new titles to suit those tastes. Some stores were less businesslike than we might have wanted them to be. I'll never forget that on a trip to Philadelphia, I dropped in to Wanamaker's department store, which had a huge book section. I'd just published Stein and Day's first book, Elia Kazan's *America America,* and neither I nor my companion could find it in the store. Finally, I asked a clerk if they had the book in stock and she led us from the fiction section over to the poetry section, where many copies of *America America* were on display. "Why here?" I asked, and the woman answered, "The title sounded so poetic."

In the twenty-first century some traditional bookstores have shriveled and died. Their competition was from large chains that stocked mainly books on the bestseller list or by previously very successful authors, and how-to books, but the accent was on sell-through commerce and infrequently on cultural importance or value. Of course newly published books for the educated reader were also on sale in some mall stores but few became standard backlist in those stores.

Children's Books and Young Adult Books

These are specialized markets as to content, size, illustrations, and vetting by children's librarians. Consequently the editors, except in the smallest publishing firms, are specialists in these fields. I learned early that children's librarians are greatly concerned about the outer dimensions of children's books because they have to fit shelves of a certain size. I recall them turning down two works of near genius, *The Magic Blot* and *A Day in the Life of a Clown,* both written and illustrated by William Archibald, which required a larger-than-usual page size for his magnificent pen and ink illustrations. Librarians protested because the books were too large for conventional shelving. Archibald's books have since been shown to children of several generations and their response to the drawings is so profound that they reluctantly turn pages.

Choosing Subjects for Nonfiction

Something you know a lot about or do well is a good place to start for articles. If thinking about a book, take a look at the books about your chosen subject or field. Also check books on related subjects. What's good about each? Is there room for the book you have in mind? How well have those books done? Which have done best and why? Check out a library copy. The library may keep a record of how many people have taken it out. If you have a friend in publishing, that friend may be able to find out discreetly if a competitive book is still selling.

Tip: The negligible or stopped sale of past books is not necessarily a sign that potential buyers are not interested in the subject. Publishers let books go out of print for diverse and sometimes stupid reasons. My very first list (for the Beacon Press in Boston) contained mostly very good books I liked that had gone out of print for no good reason. I had to buy the rights to one from a major publisher. It cost me $1,000. The book was George Orwell's *Homage to Catalonia,* which went on to become number 42 of the "100 best nonfiction books of the twentieth century." When I paid the publisher, his sales manager said, "It's like taking candy from a baby." Some candy. Some baby. There's a lot of treasure in other people's sandpits. In your library, the forgotten words of long ago will trigger thoughts of subject matter that will seem surprisingly fresh when you bring it up-to-date in your own style.

Commercial
Frequently used as an adjective for popular fiction, as in "commercial novels." "Commercial" is sometimes used to derogate some kinds of popular writing out of snobbery and possibly monetary envy. The shelf life in bookstores of commercial fiction is usually short, but can be quite profitable if it catches on or the author's previous work was successful. Writers of commercial fiction focus on alarming plots, often with a leading character who manages to survive from book to book.

Commissioned Nonfiction
This is usually done on the basis of a written proposal that has been vetted by an editor or outsider who knows the field, together with examples of writing (at least the first chapter)

that are not pedestrian. A publisher who has not published in the field of the proposed book needs to have that market examined for its successes and failures before a final determination is made. This doesn't apply to cute nonfiction books, which ought to be vetted by editors who were recently in the cute stage themselves. There are instructional books available on the writing of proposals that most first-time nonfiction authors might study profitably.

Commissioning Fiction

Don't. I would also advise editors against buying fiction that is half finished. I succumbed only once. The idea for the novel was good and the submitted first half was well written. We signed up the book. Mistake. The author was unable to get the second half right. There was mistaken pressure to go ahead anyway because the first half was good even if the second half couldn't be remedied. The book was a predictable failure, as it deserved to be. Stein and Day had a good reputation for fiction and set some records at the time, but this purchase of a novel in midstream still haunts me and warns you.

Competition

Before signing a proposed book of nonfiction, pay attention to books of the same or similar subject matter that have been published by others. This will help with pricing and promotion, but the most important purpose of this product research is to see where the proposed book fits on the list of books published elsewhere. If the book is good but clearly not as good as the leading books in the field, the new one will be risky unless it contains new material that was perhaps not available earlier, when the better books were published. An author's credentials count. Name recognition is a factor. To do a book that is okay but not as good as competing books is not recommended except for fields in which many books exist and somehow thrive. For example, some hobbyists and specialists enjoy owning every book on their subject because it gives them a sense of completeness.

Contracts, Book
When Atheneum began publishing its distinguished list in the mid-twentieth century, it used an author's contract that I recall ran two legal-size pages. It was written in polite English and was courteous and reciprocal in its presentation. Atheneum said in plain words first what it would do for the author and second what it expected the author to do to satisfy his publishing obligations. It was a gentlemen's rather than a bureaucrat's contract, and I tried to do a similar contract for Stein and Day, two sides of one legal-size page. This gradually evolved into longer contracts, and much more time was spent between editors and publishers and their house counsel. Today, twelve- and fourteen-page contracts are commonplace, going into issues most authors don't understand, which makes help from an agent almost mandatory. The negotiations, arguments, and exchanges are between agent and acquiring editor or the publisher's legal department. Some of the issues are not important. The amount of the advance and how it is paid are important, and so is the royalty rate. One point to watch out for today is large sales made to warehouse chains

and similar businesses who receive unusually high discounts and produce a lower royalty rate per book. That seems acceptable except that the royalty percentage is of the net price to the dealer whereas standard royalties relate to the list price.

Special circumstances may need to be negotiated for electronic sales, which are quite negotiable, especially if the author has previously excluded them from a former contract. Income can be derived from new subsidiary rights, including electronic rights. Traditionally what was written was sold only as a book, first hardcover, then paperback if warranted, with perhaps an early excerpt published in a magazine, and then foreign editions. A few lucky novels ended up as movies. At present the market for the written word includes recordings, handheld electronic devices, and downloads in addition to the traditional hardcover and/or paperback.

The author is entitled to free copies, the number usually specified in the contract. A usual number of the first edition of a hardcover is ten copies. If the author has special contacts in the press or other media, he may request promotion copies for such use. If an author wishes to buy additional copies of his or her book, the contract may specify the minimum number of copies for an order and the discount the author will receive. That discount may increase with higher numbers of copies. Transportation is usually the author's responsibility. Tip: Keep at least one copy of the first and any additional editions in a safe place. If you become well known, those copies increase in value over the years. Copies signed by the author may have more value. I once was vacationing with family members and my brother-in-law Jack spotted a secondhand-book store. Inside, he noticed a novel of mine in a section that had a sign saying "50¢ Books!" He bought my book and turned to me to sign it, which I did. The bookseller saw this and immediately said, "If I'd known it was going to be signed I'd have charged two dollars!"

Once an author has had a book published by trade publishers he is eligible to join the Authors Guild, which can provide him a good deal of information about contracts without charge. Its legal department will answer any questionable items or review the whole contract. That service alone is worth more than the annual fee. The Authors Guild publishes a journal four times a year for members only. It contains information and articles I have found useful year after year.

Contractual Issues

An author is entitled to a number of free copies of his work as soon as the edition has been produced. The usual number is ten copies, but experienced writers who do prepublication publicity are usually given a larger number of copies for distribution to prospective interviewers, local newspapers, and other publicity sources. The contract usually provides for the number of free copies. An author has to right to have his book published in a reasonable period of time, which may be indicated in the contract.

An author is licensing his work for an indefinite period as long as a work remains in print either with the original publisher or a sublicensee such as a paperback publisher, a CD publisher, etc. If a work goes out of print an author can demand by letter that the book be reissued within a period of time. Otherwise the license will expire and the author can take the book elsewhere if there is a continuing market for it.

Controversial Content

A nation's culture and values stem largely from parents, teachers, and books. A book is a conduit between writers whose values and beliefs are different from the beliefs or experiences of, say, industrial managers whose experience is from other fields. Publishing in the twenty-first century finds the need for these differing cultures to cooperate in a process that is really a conduit between writers and readers that requires understanding and tolerance. To put the values of others out to the world is a noble enterprise that, like the humans who make it possible, will have its ups and downs. The publishing business needs writers and writers need publishers. Unlike the book people who organized and ran the early publishing companies of the twentieth century, managers new to publishing must possess or acquire tolerance for a process that is quite different from the norm of business.

Copyediting

Should not be confused with editing. The copy editor corrects errors in grammar and spelling and appropriateness of words and phrases; copyediting is a specialized function quite different from manuscript editing and is done after the manuscript has been edited. A worthy copy editor will not only correct punctuation and grammar errors that have been overlooked by the writer and editor, but will check errant facts and sometimes supply needed corrections for sense or rhythm. A worthy copy editor is in a high station at low pay but is very necessary in the publishing process. Copy editors are a blessed breed that finds flaws in grammar, fact, rhythm, and repetition missed by the author.

D

Deadline
The date by which a manuscript is due to be delivered to the publishing firm, usually stated in the contract.

Deep Discount
One of the advantages of having a good agent rather than going it alone is the deep-discount clause that shows up in many book-publishing contracts. The very largest resellers of books, the chains and warehouse stores, negotiate higher discounts from the list price than the publisher normally allows to retailers. Author contracts can reflect this large discount by declaring that if the discount is larger than X to the retailer, the royalty will be Y, a percentage of the cost to the retailer rather than of the cover or list price. The author's take per copy sold goes down significantly if his book is the kind that will sell to the giant stores at deep discounts. Where the deep-discount royalty begins is the subject of negotiation between agent and publisher.

Delivery Date

When a nonfiction manuscript is contracted for on the basis of a proposal there is usually a date by which the manuscript must be delivered in satisfactory form to the publisher. (Actually, the manuscript goes to the assigned editor.) I've met writers who don't pay strict attention to the delivery date on the assumption that writing a book is not a mechanical process and can't necessarily be completed by a specific date. The fact is that the date is important to the publisher, who must orchestrate and plan all the facilities and procedures that are necessary for a book to be published in a certain season. As a publisher I always felt good about a book that an author delivered early, allowing more time for other needs in the publication process. Timely delivery is not just a courtesy but an obligation that an author should not treat lightly. If sickness or some other authentic reason for delay is in the cards, the assigned editor should receive some notice that there may be a delay, even if slight. Of course if the delivery is through an agent, it's a good idea to allow for the extra time of the sending and resending involved. If there are unresolved problems that you want to discuss with the editor, it might be a good idea to deal with them by e-mail or phone well before the due date to allow corrections to be made before delivery of the final manuscript. Writers sometimes overlook the fact that an editor is likely to be dealing with a number of books at the same time.

One can't really put a deadline on fiction, though contracts do. Novels and story collections are usually sold when complete, and delivery deadlines do not apply, though an editor who must do extensive rewriting will usually require the work to be finished by an agreed date.

Delivery Option for Manuscripts

Whole manuscripts with hundreds of pages can be delivered by secure mail but that is time consuming and expensive, especially to overseas publishers. More and more companies suggest sending expected manuscripts as attachments to e-mail. They are then printed at the receiving end.

Direct Mail

At one time there were more than a hundred book clubs in the United States, most of whose members were acquired through direct-mail solicitation. The great advantage of direct mail is that lists of prospective buyers could be tested with small keyed mailings. My computer programs for writers (e.g., WritePro™, FictionMaster™) were sold through direct mail in addition to coupon advertising in magazines.

The toughest direct-mail problem I had to overcome when young occurred when I worked briefly for McCann Erickson. They were trying to solicit major companies to take on their stewardship in advertising but that had to be done in person by someone high up with whom getting an appointment was like hitchhiking in the desert. As for direct mail addressed to Mr. Right, his secretary's secretary would throw such mail in the wastebasket. The number of people we wanted most to reach was relatively small. What I did was to create a facsimile of a U.S. passport. When an assistant saw the boss's photo inside that was enough to get the mailing admitted to the throne room. Of course the photographs were obtained from photos in magazines of the people we were trying to reach, which required quite a bit of research. The facsimile inside spoke of a "Passport to Direct Sales." The quick reaction from the prospect was that the people at McCann who created the mailing were smart. Frank Armstrong, my boss, would than be invited in for a discussion that might get McCann a big new client.

Direct Marketing

This is a tricky business for books because books are relatively inexpensive items and the cost of direct-mail solicitation is not cheap. An exception is a book that claims to contain a solution to a problem, such as alcoholism. As I write, direct marketing is being used for a fat book that promises solutions to practically all problems and seems directed to a relatively unsophisticated audience. However, e-mail marketing is also worth considering with more serious books for which e-mail addresses of members of the target audience can be obtained from companies specializing in that service.

E

Editing

New writers and laypersons sometimes confuse editing with copyediting (see **Copyediting**). My favorite thesaurus supplies additional meanings that are more instructive. To edit is to check, correct, improve, amend, polish, modify, revise, reword, rewrite, redraft, condense, cut, and abridge, some or all of which I have done with the manuscripts of hundreds of books. An editor is not a writer (though some few are). An editor is a reader of other people's writings, a reviser with specific aims ranging from questioning and correcting inaccuracies to improving the vocabulary or the rhythm of the drafted words. It is customary for the writer to have the final say on edited material, though long-established and experienced editors have reputations that cause writers to pay careful attention to suggestions ranging from single words to revisions that call for a new draft.

Even excellent and experienced editors fear for their lives when having to indicate that x number of pages the writer labored over are superfluous or uninteresting and the pages should be eliminated. Some editors are gentle, knowing how dear a writer's words are to the writer, but the editor is finally the protector of the reader's interest. As a writer I relied heavily on the wise but sometimes painful advice of a few editors. I owe a debt to most of them and admire their courage in editing an editor. My greatest experience as a novelist was in the hands of the late, great Tony Godwin, a friend who was once editorial director of Penguin in England and often a houseguest of mine in New York. He kicked my fiction to a higher level mercilessly, as was his intention. He apparently did much the same for the many writers who showed up at his funeral when he died at much too young an age. In the reverse direction, when I served as editor of Elia Kazan's novel *The Understudy,* we had already established our rapport over several huge theater and film successes of his. His dedication described what length a dedicated editor must go to at times: "To Sol, who saw what I didn't think possible."

The first editor of my novels had a fierce reputation as an unkind, bossy personality. He and I managed to get along largely because of my training in the infantry and my own loud voice. Subsequently at another house, I had a high-ranking editor with a timid touch, and I found myself preferring his tough predecessor.

Editorial Boards

These boards decide what new books the publishing firm will take on. Some members will likely be senior at this company and will consequently have more clout than others. It is up to whoever is in charge of the meeting to see that less-influential newcomers have a chance to make their case for or against a project being considered. An editorial board governed by a heavy hand is in danger of becoming a one-person board, which of course minimizes the advantages of different experiences and backgrounds. In my decades at the head of such a board I tried to delegate power to individual editors who had worked well in the field of a book being considered. Some if not most editorial boards require the originating editor who proposes a book to have a written document with cost and sales estimates, some of which are inevitably imaginary rather than the result of experience. In the early twentieth century and before, new projects or books were selected mainly by publishers or editors who were themselves intensive book people who relied on their own taste and experience. That era is gone, but many editorial boards have one or two editors with long experience who provide leadership in their special areas of interest or competence. The evidence of experience is often more reliable than numbers, fictitious or not, and some high-ranking publishing executives are learning that editorial judgment cannot easily be reduced to numbers.

Editor's Functions

An editor reads and evaluates manuscripts that have been submitted by reputable agents or by previously published authors. If he recommends a manuscript's acquisition to the editorial board, the manuscript will be referred to as that editor's book. Of course it is the author's work, but if accepted it will include the editor's work also. The editor functions in the author's interest by suggesting changes and improvements to the author. The editor will have had experience with many other books and authors, and, in my experience at least, contributes much to the book's value. That's true even if the editorial suggestions are minimal, because it is also the editor's responsibility to tout the book's value to management, the sales force, and the publicity and promotion department. This takes nothing away from the author, whose credit as sole author will be on the jacket and title page and in the catalog and other promotional material. In the best relationships, the editor and the author are like members of a tight team working for the book's success. In several instances, the editors of my books became good friends. The same is true of instances when I switched roles and edited a book for the publishing firm I headed. The writing of the book is solely the author's work. The process of editing and publishing the book is the work of a tight small team.

David Brooks once said that in the nineteenth century maturity was reached when an individual conquered his inner depravity; in the twentieth century maturity involved young people's search for inner identity rather than self-mastery; and in the twenty-first century there has been yet another shift in young people—maturity is now measured by service to others. If so, editing should be on the rise, for an editor's work is to service the writer's work, to help the writer achieve his (the writer's) intent. What Brooks didn't say was that some authors do not deliver their manuscripts on time, that editors must be sensitive to the peculiar situation of the writer who sits alone in a room facing a computer, revealing for eventual public scrutiny his knowledge, passions, obsessions, and fears. The editor is the writer's sympathetic and knowledgeable sounding board. He learns to empathize with the author's moods and irrationalities, and lends the lone worker encouragement, hope, and support.

Electronic Rights

This is a contract point that covers sales of written material (formerly known as books) in digital form, usually through downloading, often done through a third party. The royalty per copy is usually lower than for a physical book, but the volume for some titles can be considerable given the reach of the Internet.

F

Fair Use
The copyright law permits relatively brief passages of copyrighted material to be used in other works. For example, a brief quotation from a previously published book by someone else can be used in a new book by another author under the "fair use" doctrine. Quotations in reviews and scholarly works are permitted. Beyond fair use, excerpts require approval by the original publisher and author.

First Serial Rights
Rights licensed to a magazine or newspaper for use of some part of a book prior to the publication in book form. This is solicited by book publishers for its promotion value as well as for the payment.

Foreign Sales, Fiction
I apologize to all non-American readers of this book by assuming for this explanation that the first publisher to sign up a given work is based in the United States. Beginning writers seldom are aware of the extent of the foreign market for their books. Most American agents have subagents in the major foreign markets and split the agency percentage. For Americans, the British market is important given the common language (though there *are* differences!), but the German market can be more rewarding financially. In my experience, Australia has a special appetite for American fiction, perhaps

because it, too, is a relatively new nation. The French market is difficult to estimate because the culture is high and special. One of the most difficult markets for Americans is Russia, though one of my novels did end up on the Moscow bestseller list. Payment was made in a strange way. I can say no more.

Italian publishers are the only ones I know who will print three editions of a novel simultaneously, each with a different jacket aiming at a different audience. My Italian publisher does something that might well be copied by publishers elsewhere. A novel of mine, published in the United States and UK as *Other People*, was published in Italy with three very different jackets. The trade edition of *Gli Altri* has on its jacket front a tasteful color photograph of a beautiful woman in an open wrap, her breasts visible. It is an enchanting jacket, clearly meant to arouse at least the curiosity of the upscale reader. It is dignified and beautiful. An edition by the Club Italiano dei Lettori has an entirely different audience in mind. The jacket has three faces of a single man over the knocked-down body of a woman, the entire scene driven by a sense of activity. A third edition, for the Club degli Editori, goes way down in class for its active jacket of a man's oversize hands grasping the clothed body of a screaming woman. To continue the emphasis, the title is large and at an angle, the whole smacking of pulp violence, though the novel itself was directed to a relatively upscale reader.

Fiction that is very successful on U.S. bestseller lists can get translated into many languages, but transactions will usually be done through subagents.

Foreign Sales, Nonfiction

Americans have a large appetite for instructional books, but many of them are not readily salable to foreign publishers. However, books with special interests may appeal to readers in other countries who know English and can afford to buy American books. Some instructional books have had surprisingly large markets abroad. Nonfiction on subjects with international interest is published in translation. For instance, I've been very lucky with *Stein on Writing* and *How to Grow a Novel* in Germany. The second title was not a good one for Britain because they don't use the American expression of growing something in the same way, so the British publisher called it *Solutions for Novelists*. Since American books are available online to British writers, some have bought two copies of the same book because of the different titles. I suggest that writers and editors give some thought to titles in translation. This is one of the things to think about early.

Format for Manuscripts

This applies to fiction or nonfiction that is being prepared for submission to publishers or publications. Many newcomers to writing sabotage their work by writing in a format that looks "unprofessional" to editors. Never ever decorate a manuscript.

Paper Size: For book-length manuscripts, even partial manuscripts, use standard paper 11 inches high and 8.5 inches wide and print on only one side of the page.

Margins: One-inch margins on both sides and top and bottom of the page are commonplace.

Line Spacing: Double-space all manuscripts and use only one side of the page. In fiction, moving to a new scene can be indicated by skipping four lines. For nonfiction, an important quote of several sentences may be set with narrower margins.

Chapter Headings: These should be centered at the top of a new page. Do not start a new chapter in the middle of a page.

Page Numbering: For fiction especially I recommend numbering the pages in the middle bottom of the page, making it less visible to the reader turning pages. You don't want the reader noticing the page number while immersed in what you have to say. The middle bottom offers the least interference in the reader's experience of your work. Page numbers can be an unhelpful intrusion if placed, say, in the upper right, where they will be noticed.

Title Page: *Beneath a centered title,* "By" sometimes precedes the author's name in manuscript but is always deleted in the book. Larger-than-normal type for a title or an author's name is often thought to indicate that the manuscript is from an amateur. Boldface for the title is okay. In the lower left corner, put your name on the first line, and beneath it in two lines with your address, then an e-mail address if you have one. If you have an agent, the agent will replace your information with the agent's own name, the agency name if relevant, address, etc. in that lower left corner of the title page.

Paper Quality: Twenty-pound white paper is acceptable. I use a 20-pound paper with a 96 brightness rating. A 28-pound paper with a brightness of 97 or better may be more suitable for some manuscripts if they are expected to receive more than usual handling. The heavier paper of course costs more, and also costs more to ship or mail.

Typeface: The typeface you choose is important. I strongly suggest a serif typeface, i.e., one with little curlicues on the letters whose function is to link the letters of each word. *We read words not separate letters.* Sans serif (without curlicues) typefaces are okay for headlines and some kinds of advertising copy, and take slightly less space. Use a standard, common typeface like Times New Roman. Twelve-point is the right size. Your aim should be to have the manuscript look professional.

Freelance Editors

Experienced editors no longer working for publishing companies sometimes turn to freelance work, helping writers—usually with finished drafts of fiction or nonfiction—to perfect their work and improve the chances for publication. There are some very experienced editors doing this kind of work. Writers find them on the Web or through other writers. Some freelance editors have bonded together in organizations and companies. Freelance editors charge by the length of the manuscript or by the hour. Checking out the kinds of books that freelancers have worked on previously is a necessity.

G

Genre
A category of books by subject matter and sometimes by style, tone, and literary quality or its absence. In publishing jargon the genre title for detective stories and their kin is *crime*. The collective name for works of action/suspense is *thriller*. Science fiction and fantasy are popular genres, particularly among younger readers. Memoirs are a genre, and so are autobiographies and biographies. The number of categories has grown: books of African American interest have become a genre. So have gay market books. History, biography, and computer books are all genres. By and large novels of significant literary value are less subject to categorization, as are an increasing number of venturesome nonfiction books that are for the moment sui generis or unique.

H

Handle
In publishing, a short, usually one-sentence, characterization of a book. It is used most often by book salesmen in a thirty-second presentation to a bookseller. It is advantageous for an author to compose a short handle for his or her work early. It should be sent to the editor after the manuscript has been accepted. There is an art to writing handles.

I

Interview Tips

I learned this from one of my authors, Elia Kazan. If you're doing a TV interview, sit with your backside as far back as it will go against the back of the chair. *It forces you to project.* Try it. It works.

You can't rely on your interviewer to ask the right questions, but prepare yourself to give the right answers that will get readers interested in your book. When asked a question whose answer is useless for your purpose, this is not time for your usual politeness; quickly provide a practiced answer. In most instances the interviewer will be glad because his or her job is to fill the air with material that will interest listeners, and if you do that your way, it's fine.

For a TV interview try to imagine (after all, you do work with your imagination) how viewers would expect you to dress and try to fit that model if you can. If you're a relaxed sort of guy, don't wear a tie as you would for a wedding. Dress informally. Save your formal clothes for when you accept the Nobel Prize.

Warning: This one is for editors, publishers, and publicists. If you're an author, please don't read this paragraph. One of the authors I published was the British prime minister Edward Heath, who was a phlegmatic public speaker. I had lined up a CBS interview for him and arranged for us to arrive early at a place close to the interview site, where I showed the prime minister a video called something like *The Decline and Fall of Britain*. He watched it for ten or fifteen minutes, growing increasingly angry and red in the face, and finally said, "Enough!" I said, "Good, we're just in time for the press conference next door." The phlegmatic speaker gave a rousing interview in defense of England. He was a smart man, of course, and complimented me afterward for raising his temperature before he spoke to the press.

Inventory

This is a confession of fault and a warning to new publishers and watchful small publishers. At many board meetings of Stein and Day, one or another director would raise the issue of inventory. A portion of our backlist sold slowly but continually. A larger portion comprised books that were essentially in storage, having lived there 99 percent of their lives. Someone calculated that remaindering that amount would bring in a few million dollars of working capital for publication of new books. But as a publisher who was also a book lover, I resisted, supported by an anecdote about a worthwhile book that had an initial sale mainly to libraries. Seven years after its publication, a nationally syndicated medical columnist wrote a piece about the book, and within days the orders cleaned out our stock. I think the directors tired of hearing that anecdote used to justify retaining slow-moving or paralyzed backlist inventory. The commercial warehouse in which our inventory was stored was not in a rainless part of the country, and one day a ferocious storm struck the roof of the warehouse in which the bulk of our inventory was kept. That roof had glass panes in the ceiling that couldn't withstand the ferocity of the storm. They burst. Insurance covered only a small part of the loss.

I shamefully record this warning to young publishers lest they, like me, love books too much. A much better practice is to use one's love of books to resuscitate the worthy books that other publishers let go out of print too fast.

J

Jacket Copy
Most hardcover books will have copy on both the front and back flaps of the jacket. That copy originates with the editor or publicity department. A few authors with experience in the publishing world may be able to write their own jacket copy, but most writers can't hack it, because they are too close to the material or don't understand the purpose of the jacket well enough. It is not just to keep a hardcover book in mint condition as long as possible. The purpose of front flap copy should be to entice a casual reader to look at the first pages of the book. At the same time, for nonfiction, the front jacket copy should make it clear what this book offers the reader (that's where the author himself often goes wrong because authors are too likely to indulge in favorable adjectives or hyperbole). The back flap provides several different kinds of opportunity. If the author has published previous books that had a significant audience, that's possibly the place to remind a reader of the author's earlier work, in words that

will entice attention to the current work. For a first book, it is essential to use the jacket for conveying the author's credentials to write on the subject. Photographs of the author are useful if the author is at all interesting looking.

K

Keeping in Touch

A century or more ago, it was customary for editors and sometimes publishers to keep in touch with their authors. They knew the author's work, family, and other circumstances, and in a few cases friendships blossomed that lasted a lifetime. As I write, publishing companies are more like other companies, bigger and more impersonal. Yet close relations continue to exist especially between editors and their authors. This has a benefit to both sides. Authors are inclined to stick with their editors when circumstances permit and vice versa.

Because publishing is a worldwide business, relations can also be established with agents, editors, and publishers in other countries where the author's work is translated.

Kill Fee

Applies to articles, not books, commissioned but not published. The fee is a percentage of the agreed price if published.

L

Lecturing

As originally practiced in the nineteenth century, lecturing is passé. Charles Dickens is said to have developed the practice of reading work aloud as public-platform entertainment. He allegedly brought the idea to America from England along about 1867. The auditoriums were packed and in one season he is said to have earned $200,000. Dickens read scenes from his books. He read with excessive energy and it was like an acting turn as much as a reading. Mark Twain said, "When Providence had had enough of that kind of crime the Authors' Readings ceased from troubling and left the world at peace."

Lecturing was an earlier occupation and different from reading. The author didn't read from notes, or a manuscript, or a book. After learning what he was to say by heart, perhaps with an occasional quick look at a cheat sheet, he would declaim his words to paying audiences. Lecturing was at the height of its popularity just after the Civil War and has persisted on and off since, with lecture bureaus (agents for speakers) arranging for authors to speak to existing groups. Mark Twain was not happy lecturing. He discovered that well-written pages were not for speech. Their form is literary. Writings do not lend themselves to happy and effective delivery where their purpose is merely to entertain. He said, "They have to be limbered up, broken up, colloquialized, and turned into common forms of premeditated talk—otherwise they will bore the house, not entertain it." After a while, Twain learned to extemporize to suit the occasion, becoming a storyteller instead of a writer.

Legal Issues

Avoiding problems for nonfiction calls for due diligence, a term that implies a careful examination of an author's credentials, previous books and/or articles, and reputation in his field, if applicable. Permissions are required for the use of lengthier material from copyrighted sources. A review by house counsel or outside attorney is in order if the manuscript involves material that is actionable if incorrect. Cookbooks and books with health advice require special care. For fiction, the editor needs to watch out for possible use of real names of people, companies, stores, etc. Some asserted facts may need to be checked or clarified. Authors who are members of the Authors Guild can inquire about potential issues to the legal department of the Guild. For publishers it is advantageous to have outside counsel from a lawyer familiar with copyright and other publishing issues.

Letters

Letters to agents and publishing firms should always be addressed to an individual by name. If you don't know the name, your library probably has a current copy of the annual *LMP* (*Literary Market Place*), which contains the names of editors and agents as well as addresses and other contact information.

Library Sales

Sales to libraries are deemed important mainly because new books to libraries are rarely returned. American libraries as a whole can be counted on for an advance purchase of several thousand copies of a new hardback. Librarians order books in advance of publication based on subject interest, an author's prior success measured by the number of times a book is taken out of a library, and mostly by advance reviews of new adult books. This underpinning helps publishers speculate on the number of copies to be ordered for the first printing for books likely to have a slow sale over time to book buyers. The following journals should receive information about, and a bound galley of, a forthcoming book well in advance. Each journal should be checked for the date by which it wants bound galleys for review.

> *Library Journal,* 249 W. 17th St., New York, NY 10011
>
> *Booklist,* American Library Association, 50 E. Huron St., Chicago, IL 60611
>
> *Kirkus Reviews,* 200 Park Ave. S., New York, NY 10003
>
> *Publishers Weekly,* 71 W. 23rd St. Suite 1608, New York, NY 10010

Some librarians rely on reviews in *The New York Times Book Review,* which is available by subscription prior to its general distribution with the newspaper.

Library distributors accommodate books published by smaller firms.

Life After Death: An Insider's Tale

Stein and Day once had a sales manager named Malcolm Magruder, who was a lovable genius with bookstore buyers, especially women. I and others would sometimes stop to listen to him talking to a buyer on the phone about a forthcoming visit and the wonderful new books he was to tell her about. Needless to say, the accounts he personally called upon stocked our books well.

Before Magruder I had my druthers about publishing salespeople based on my first venture into the trade. As an interested outsider I was astonished when Bertram Wolfe's masterpiece *Three Who Made a Revolution* was quickly put out of print by its original publisher after it sold only a thousand or so copies. Anchor Books had just launched and I knew a couple of people at the top, and I went to see the person I knew I wanted this particular book to see back in print. But Anchor's books at the outset were smaller than hardcover books, and the editor I talked to said Wolfe's masterpiece would take three volumes, each of which would have to sell something like thirty-seven thousand copies just to break even. One morning soon thereafter I stepped out of the shower with an idea: Why not paperbacks the same size as hardcover books? I called Melvin Arnold, head of the Beacon Press in Boston, with whom I had a book that was thirteen weeks on the *New York Times* bestseller list, and gave me some credence. I quickly told him my idea. Before my egg timer hit the three-minute mark he said he was headed for the airport to hop a plane for New York. He hired me as an outside editor, the first such assignment in my career. At the next semiannual sales meeting, the salesmen spoke against the concept of book-size paperbacks. They complained that softcover books were supposed to be pocket books and these books wouldn't fit in a pocket! They said the books didn't look American! The French were putting out paperbacks in book size. And so forth. It can be assumed that Mel Arnold was a publisher of the old school. He ignored the salesmen's naysaying and went forward with the program, which proved to be a gold mine of sorts.

The book-size paperback of *Three Who Made a Revolution* sold a half a million copies and was adopted by most Russian studies courses in the country. Here are the other books I was able to put into book-size paperbacks in the first season:

> *Homage to Catalonia* by George Orwell (later chosen as one of the hundred best nonfiction books of the century).
>
> *An End to Innocence,* Leslie Fiedler's first book. Later, at Stein and Day, I published seventeen of his books.
>
> *The Need for Roots* by Simone Weil, preface by T. S. Eliot.
>
> *The Hero in History* by Sidney Hook.
>
> *Social Darwinism in American Thought* by Richard Hofstadter.
>
> *The Invisible Writing* by Arthur Koestler.

This proves that some books chosen carefully can have a life after death. Eventually the book-size paperback became the standard paperback format pretty much everywhere.

Location

The majority of American publishers are located in New York City just as the majority of British publishers are located in London. Just before the Civil War there were 112 publishers in New York. A few were in Boston and Philadelphia. By the twentieth century, there were a few publishers in the Midwest and California, with small publishing operations popping up in other parts of the country. Agents are everywhere, but again New York has the majority. It is not a coincidence that a large number of writers live in and around New York City.

M

Management

In the early years of American publishing, the management of publishing firms could be counted on to be book people who treasured the well-written word and who didn't have a calculator on their desk. The managers were interested in writing for its own sake, all of which sounds very unbusinesslike, but those publishers were also businessmen, and some of the companies they founded became large enterprises in their hands. At this writing, those beliefs are held mainly by devout editors who are the essential link between the creative act of writing and the business of publishing. Writers honor them. The work of writers and editors is the ultimate source of what the business achieves for its shareholders. And, in a literary house, it achieves honor for its constituency.

Marketing Timetable

It is said that in summertime people prefer to read light novels on vacation. Some do, some don't. Some books seem destined to be presents, but that doesn't mean that they should be published before the Christmas season. A book needs time to become known through reviews and comments from early readers.

Mass-Market Books

Refers to inexpensive paperback books sold in airports, bus stations, newspaper kiosks, hotels, and supermarkets, usually in racks, with the books' front covers visible. The majority of such books interest travelers and avid readers of popular material. Each season some become big bestsellers. In times past, competition for popular titles by mass-market publishers caused such books to be auctioned by the originating publisher, which contributed greatly to the original publisher's bottom line (and the author's also). The guarantees and subsequent royalties paid to the originating publishers were usually a considerable portion of their profit. Later, publishers acquired their own mass-market imprints.

Midlist

Long ago I was asked to write an article about this hairy subject and to my chagrin it qualified me as an expert on a subject that I wouldn't want to talk about on a day when the sun was shining. For every publishing season (some publishers have two seasons a year, some three) decisions are made ahead of time that will greatly influence both the writer's and the publisher's economic life. If a superlarge advance was paid for a book, you can be damn sure it will be at the top of the list for its publishing season, or in second place if another book had a huge advance, because the publishing hierarchy not only wants to recoup the advance paid but hopes that a blockbuster bestseller will make up for books on the list that don't come anywhere near their expectations. Moreover, the promotion plans for a season, including advertising and publicity costs, are allocated mainly to such books because books do not sell if readers don't know they exist. Reviews help, but as I write, book review media have been dwindling.

So the publisher has a list on top of which are one or two titles. They are the books that a publishing salesman walking into a bookstore will mean when he announces to the buyer, "Hey, what till you see what I have for you!" They are called door openers. Sales executives will have visited the appropriate chain buyers early to get a commitment and to pay for upfront display space if it is available and required for a large buy.

At the bottom of the season's list are books that will sell mainly to libraries and may tempt a small number of aficionados, including the author's parents if they are still alive. Everything between the top and bottom is considered midlist. There are exceptions. When Oprah Winfrey picked a book for her on-air book club, its place on the list was transformed; the publisher printed a million copies and had the publicity department working overtime contacting their contacts.

For the salesmen in the field, the midlist gives them an opportunity to play personal favorites. If a salesman served in the war with a certain division or in a certain territory and that's the subject of the book, he'll be sure to talk it up during his visit. If the subject of the book is close to the heart of Texas and Texas is in the salesman's territory, you know what happens. The book gets talked about during the sales session, which may cost other books on the midlist their lives, but the Texas book will make up for it.

Now for the tragic point. The midlist is large and the bookstore buyer's time (or the salesman's) is short, and books get skipped. So there are really two screenings of every manuscript, the first when it is submitted and the second when it is supposed to be talked about during the salesman's visit.

Multiple Queries
These are queries sent simultaneously to several publishers, presenting a brief prospectus of a book project or manuscript. This applies most to specialized nonfiction.

Multiple Submissions
Publishers' Web sites and some publishing reference works will state the type of submission required (e.g., not via e-mail) and whether multiple submissions will be welcome. Some agents will not read a sample of your work if it has been sent to other agents at the same time. The principle is this: Agents and publishing editors are busy people who have an enormous amount of daily eyestrain. They don't want to be wasting their time. A writer is better off using an agent who will know the habits as well as the requirements of individual editors and publishing firms.

N

Nature of the Publishing Business
Now that businessmen run publishing establishments, it behooves them to recognize that a publishing firm is a middleman between writers who create manuscripts and readers who desire to read what's written. The business needs writers and writers need publishers. A nation's culture and values stem largely from parents, teachers, and books. To put values out to the world is a noble enterprise that, like the humans who make it possible, has its ups and downs.

Nonfiction, Commissioned
In past decades editors would more frequently than at present get ideas for books and find a writer whose experience would be appropriate for the subject. At this writing, the downturn in book publishing keeps many editors busy hanging on to the trapeze of their employment and this has contributed to lack of time to initiate such projects.

O

Option
The contractual right of a publisher to have a first look and the opportunity to bid on the author's next manuscript. An option also requires the publisher to bid—if he decides he wants to publish the work—in a specified period of time. If a

writer produces both fiction and nonfiction, the option may be limited to the category of the current work. A strong relationship between author and editor may often be more important than a legal option.

A publisher will almost always require an option on the author's next work. The terms of the option will be in the contract. There may be restrictions; for example, the option may be for the next novel but not for a nonfiction work.

P

Packagers

Sometimes called producers because their work in publishing resembles in some respects the work that producers do with plays. The packager is a person or small company that originates ideas for books, finds appropriate authors, and has necessary illustrations made. This project is then "packaged" and presented to an appropriate publisher. The royalty income is shared by contract between the packager and the author and sometimes, if warranted, illustrators. When the packaging business started up in the twentieth century, most packaged books were coffee-table books, larger than usual size with lots of illustrative material. Packaging has grown and includes many types of books, including reference books and series books. The publisher who buys the package does the usual promotion and distribution geared to the specific subject. Working with a good packager may be an easier procedure than total self-publishing for certain kinds of books. It is sometimes described as co-publishing.

Book packagers sometimes have marketing savvy for untraditional markets, for instance, selling sports books to sports outlets and chains. They are sometimes skilled also in books that require a lot of illustration. They know how to acquire rights for use of the material and how to manufacture books that depend greatly on their illustrations.

Pen Names

There are few reasons for a writer to publish under an invented name. If you are ashamed of your work, why publish it? If you publish too much, you might want to invent a pseudonym. As a publisher, I didn't welcome pseudonyms, because you can't put a pseudonymous writer on TV (radio is okay) or have him do signings at bookstores. Samuel Clemens chose Mark Twain because in his occupation as a riverboat pilot, the most favorable outcry was "Mark twain." Stephen King published one novel under his pseudonym Richard Bachman, which earned him a review that described the work as "what Stephen King would write like, if Stephen King could really write." It wasn't fair.

A longtime friend of mine, a fourth-generation American of Italian extraction, was fed up when he heard himself described as an Italian American. He said, "Isn't American good enough?" He published—this is true, believe me!—one hundred well-crafted books under non-Italian-sounding pseudonyms. Doris Lessing wrote *The Diaries* under the name Jane Somers. John Steinbeck, whom I knew for only the length of a one longish phone call, published his collected poems under the ghastly pseudonym Amnesia Glasscock, the invention of which is not to his credit if you look at the pseudonym carefully.

Press Kits and Presentation Folders

These are created by publicists to interest media people in an author's new work in the hope of getting an interview. The point to remember is that the most important interview possibilities are with people who decide quickly, which means everything should be aimed at the objective of getting an interview for the author. Controversy can help enlist some interviewers. A photograph helps. Previous successful appearances help even more. Some quotable short (and possibly amusing) views of a topic in the air can help enlist some interviewers. Some publicists outline topics suitable for a given author.

The person preparing a presentation kit should work in front of a clock with a second hand as a reminder that he is planning to seduce a very busy person. Consider that the interviewer wants to fill airtime and to do the least amount of work in preparation. If the interviewer enjoys the idea, that helps. The trade-off is the interviewee getting his book message on the air. It will come as no surprise to experienced publicity people that many authors don't have PR experience and would benefit from professional know-how about the kinds of things in their books or subject matter that can be succinct, entertaining, instructive, perhaps controversial, and perhaps stated amusingly. An author needs to be briefed and rehearsed if that is feasible. (If he lives at a distance, he might still have a working telephone!) Most authors, particularly first-timers, do not have a list of interviews they've done successfully, but even one counts if it has some prestige. See **Stunts Sell Books,** where I talk about how one TV interview on a syndicated show came to be used in many other cities. Also see **Publicity and Promotion.**

Prestige

There's no ducking the fact that book publishing is still a prestigious business. When being introduced to strangers, one doesn't always want to announce that one is a lawyer or even a judge because it produces instant thoughts that may relate to the listener's experience. If you're introducing a doctor, people normally assume you are introducing a medical personage, always assumed to be helpful in an emergency. But introduce a person as a book publisher, and watch the eyes of others, because despite the economic hazards of the business, publishing still exudes prestige just as an elaborate library was thought to do in times past. The same applies to authors of books, as if writing were something greater than many other occupations because of the prestige attached to books.

Proposals

A proposal for marriage is probably easier to do than a first-time proposal for a book. Formal proposals are for nonfiction. Editors rarely if ever buy fiction from a proposal or a brief sample. The most important ingredient is usually a factual and realistic assessment of whom the book is meant for and the size of the prospective audience, plus the author's credentials for writing to that audience. A proposal from an agent is welcome because the agent will have screened the proposal carefully and may have asked for revisions based on the agent's experience. Face it, the agentless slush pile of often poorly put-together proposals is viewed by a busy editor as a nuisance. Editors reportedly get as many as twenty-five proposals a week. Seeing if any are worth the time for a careful reading is often a discouraging experience for the editor. A proposal should contain a good title, a brief description of the proposed book, a description of its proposed audience, the competition in the market, an outline, and perhaps a very few sample pages. For beginners, it's a difficult task. There are books on the market that have sample proposals and instructions for preparing your own. Don't exaggerate or pat yourself on the back; stick to factual statements. A little human verve and spring in the writing help; factual writing doesn't need to be dull. For an editor, a good proposal can brighten a day.

Publicity and Promotion

These terms are sometimes used interchangeably, but they have different meanings. Publicity means calling public attention and interest to a new book and can include the efforts by the author if he or she is willing and able to go on radio and TV, create and keep up a blog on the Web, or simply deliver talks to small groups at bookstores. The national tour of yesteryear can now be conducted from a single location, but this is expensive and generally reserved for "blockbuster" books by writers with a national reputation or who are celebrities in some field. The purpose of using the author for publicity is to sell the book, and that's where training comes in. Take the instance of a woman down south who was quite widely known and who assumed that was all she needed was to go big-time on tour. We organized a minor TV show in New York City with a private dinner afterward to critique her performance (gently). It's very easy to lose track of your purpose once you are on the air or being taped. An author engaging with the public on television needs to know well the points she wants to get across, whether or not she is asked an appropriate question. There's a skill to getting your message across no matter what you are asked. This is not impoliteness, an interview is an exchange, filling in airtime for the interviewer in exchange for the author's access to the audience. In this case a long evening's dinner resulted in a perfect performance, and her book was a big hit mainly as a result of TV publicity. Thereafter the head of a much larger publishing house offered the author a much higher advance than we had paid for her first book. She took her next book there. She received no additional training in preparation for book two, which had a different subject and required a different take on publicity, but she was not rehearsed and the book sold poorly compared to the first book. What I'm pushing for here is skilled preparation for interviews on mass media. If an interview is not prepared for, it has all the hazards of a blind date—before an audience of millions.

However, take a television star like David Frost. His first series on television in the United States did not survive for long. Nevertheless I met his agent at a dinner party in London and took David Frost on for his book *The English*. We created an event that launched him in the United States and took his book to the number 2 spot on the bestseller list. Frost was on camera five or six nights a week in England and before he made his debut in the States. I had to whet the appetite of the publicity media in New York. Prior to publication, he was able to come over for a single day. I had him booked for the *Today* show and *The Tonight Show* on the same day. When he finished the first show, for which we had no preparation time, he was surrounded by his entourage bursting with praise. I was coming from a different direction and Frost grabbed my sleeve and said, "How did I do?" I said, "You blew it." He had been an athlete at Cambridge and was driven to succeed. He pulled me into a nearby room that was empty of people, where I was able to tell him in private that he had a terrific reputation as the king of British television but what he was supposed to be doing was selling his book *The English*. We ended up in his hotel suite, where we had heavy talk until it was time to go for the taping of *The Tonight Show*. When he excused himself for the necessary, his girlfriend came out of the bedroom to say, "You can't talk to David Frost that way!" I told her the investment was mine also. Frost was a very quick study, and the upshot was a bang-up book publicity event that evening that sent a lot of people to bookstores. I mention this incident to point out to writers that even experienced TV interviewers need training in how to get a particular book across on TV. Laymen authors need more preparation.

Books whose substance can be of interest to the public have a chance at newspaper interviews, which are quite different from TV interviews. Journalists are more interested in subject matter that might appeal to their audience. The author can have a relaxed time answering questions but should not get far off the subject, because an interviewer has a lot to do in a day and often hasn't chitchat time. The interviewer might be a very interesting person, but he has to get on with his work, so it pays to know the substance you want to get across and get the most interesting points in early.

Public radio and television are important for promotion because they tend to have an upscale audience that buys books. For what writers did in the pretelevision era, see **Lecturing.**

Promotion often refers to efforts not involving the author personally. It includes advance reading copies for major booksellers and chains, cheat sheets for sales representatives with quick points to get across, bound galleys in advance to reviewers that might produce useful quotes, getting quotes from other authors known to the public, for major books a possible appearance at a sales meeting, and advertising if the budget allows it.

Publicity, the Writer's Role
This mainly applies to nonfiction. If you're up on topical issues in the field your book deals with and you are able to talk entertainingly as well as seriously about the subject from a news point of view, the publisher's publicity department can try to get you airtime on radio and, rarely, TV. Before appearing you should listen to the given program sufficient times to get to know the kind of comment that seems to attract the

moderator or producer. Make a list of the points you'd want to make. Provocative and newsworthy points are most desirable. You also need to learn how to answer questions entertainingly. A lot depends on your personality and what makes you comfortable. In any event you need to prepare yourself to sidetrack a question to which you don't know an answer or that for some reason you don't want to answer. If you're witty or clever that will help. Most broadcasters won't mind if you don't give a straight answer to a question. Their job is to fill airtime between commercials and you're helping them.

Touring is prohibitively expensive. Be honest with yourself about your capabilities for public performance. I once had a male author who wrote a sexy book, but I watched his first TV interview and found the blandness of his personality was counterproductive for the subject of the book. My colleagues agreed that his personality was inconsistent with the material he'd written and that he came across blah. We unhappily had to cancel the rest of the tour. The audience will rise to your book because of your command of the subject matter but also because of your personality.

All publishers are not equal when it comes to publicity. In some instances, it may pay for the author to hire a publicist for both educational purposes and to help a busy publicity department at the publishing company. Not all publicists have equal contacts with publicity outlets or are good at pitching a variety of book subjects and authors. An author's self-preparation is essential. Know what makes people laugh or smile in relation to your book. Practice on friends. Practice before a recording machine you can play back. Just as some actors are make-believe authors (their books ghostwritten by others), an author needs to be a bit of an entertainer to succeed in promotion interviews for television and radio. Newspaper interviewers are another matter. If your book is important on a specific subject, be serious but light, use anecdotal material if appropriate, polish your anecdotes to make the interview enjoyable for the reporter. It will get you a better story.

Publishing Is a Business

However, it is not quite like most businesses. In the early twentieth century book publishing in America and elsewhere was often a business based on individuals who loved books more than vegetables and enjoyed the company and work of writers. Their colleagues were usually working editors who specialized as the firms grew. Publishers were a community, alternating camaraderie and jealousy with their peers. Random House, today a giant conglomerate of a firm owned by Europeans, was the baby of its founders, Bennett Cerf and Donald Klopfer. Cerf used to come to Stein and Day launching parties "to steal authors" on a quite friendly basis.

It worked both ways. Maurice Edelman, talented British novelist and MP, published several books with Random House. On his visits to the United States he was given a black-tie dinner party. What the author wanted was to have his books succeed in a big way. One day the author's British publisher handed me a copy of that author's new manuscript as I was headed for a day or two of meetings in Paris. I spent the whole first day in Paris reading *Disraeli in Love*.

I loved the book and quickly signed it up. It was the author's first book to sell a huge number of copies and make a lot of money. On my next visit to London, the happy author threw a dinner party for me at the House of Commons with invitations to "Authors who have the wrong American publisher." It was a day when small firms like Stein and Day could compete successfully against giants because the individuals and relationships counted. I got my comeuppance in Jamaica at a retreat frequented by publishers. My partner, Patricia Day, and I had arrived a day earlier. We spotted Donald Klopfer of Random House and his wife across the dance floor at their table. I went over to greet them, and Donald, seeing me, rose from his seat and in a loud voice said, "You stole Maurice Edelman from us!" His wife berated him and within minutes an apology was forthcoming and we were treated to predinner drinks for the rest of our stay, paid for by Random House.

The big change later in the twentieth century was the aggregation of companies; Random bought Knopf, until then an excellent husband-and-wife business, and today it is a huge operation owned by businesses in other countries. Financiers, CEOs, and bean counters control many of today's publishing operations and numbers rule more than taste. The intimacy and joy of finding a new author or new book have diminished. Most attention is paid to "big books," meaning those that will quickly have big sales. Love has slipped out of the business. When the business cycle turns downward, so does publishing, and what used to be a lifelong devotion is vulnerable. The strength of publishing new work is such that even in a less-friendly environment, there are people still ready to devote their lives to the business that is so unlike and more personal than other businesses, raising authors' babies as if they were one's own.

Q

Quality Paperbacks

The original paperbacks were mainly popular books reprinted on cheap paper and sold mainly through vendors of magazines. Quality paperbacks were designed to appeal to upscale readers and were printed on acid-free paper, with cover designs that expressed the literary content often without illustration of any kind. Those quality paperbacks revolutionized the paperback market. Jason Epstein bears the honor of having launched Anchor Books, which published quality books that fit into one's pocket. I bear the responsibility for launching book-size quality paperbacks, which allowed important books of length to be published, books that would not then fit the model of Anchor Books. At the first sales meeting of Beacon Paperbacks the salesmen protested that paperbacks were supposed to be pocket books and the book-size paperbacks wouldn't fit in the pocket! They also decried the fact that one of the books on the first list had a price of $2.95! Nobody, they swore, would pay that much for a paperback!

R

Remainders

Think "leftovers." A publisher may have printed too many copies of a book originally or is later inundated with returns, or an in-print book has stopped selling, or is selling too slowly to maintain in an active inventory. Quantities of such books—usually most or all—are sold to the remainder market. That's when you see a hardcover or trade paperback selling at a fraction of its original price. A big contributor to remaindering is a publisher's or editor's speculative enthusiasm for a title that ends up selling only a part of its printing.

The majority of remainders are attributable to the fact that books are never really bought by the bookseller until they are sold for good to a member of the public. Otherwise, the book can be returned to the publisher for credit. In my decades as a publisher I had a weakness. If I fell in love with a particular book, I would hesitate, sometimes for years, to remainder it. I loved a lot of books, which left me with a large but slow-selling backlist inventory. Sometimes there can be a surprise, as when a columnist or other journalist or anyone with a big name discovers a book belatedly and says so publicly; then a nearly dead title can suddenly take off and is not remaindered.

A lot of fuel is spent getting books from publishers to bookstores and from bookstores back to publishers. The business cries out for sanity. Some publishers will arrange for a title to be "remaindered in place," that is sold at a steep discount by the retailer, who is given significant credit toward his original purchase price of the book.

Returning Advances

Unearned advances do not have to be returned to the publisher, but failure to deliver a satisfactory final manuscript may require a return of the advance. I can't recall a single instance of such a return from my twenty-seven years as a publisher, though I once signed up the first half of a novel, which was quite good, and got stuck with a second half that was a clunker, which changed the rules in the firm: A novel had to be finished before a contract was issued.

Returns

The practice of allowing retailers to return unsold books for full credit came about in the Depression in the early 1930s when booksellers were loath to buy books by unknown or new authors. The firm of Simon & Schuster started the practice of crediting bookseller returns against future payments for other books.

Review Quotes

This is an important process that is often done incorrectly. I've seen ads and promotion copy that do nothing for a book. For example, "Excellent" doesn't mean much unless the person saying it has an immediately recognizable famous name, famous to the audience for the book. In nonfiction, a quote on the content and readability is desirable. Beware of overused adjectives.

The experience of reading sometimes works well. "I've read this book in one sitting and I can't wait to read it again because . . ."

Saul Bellow read half of a manuscript of a novel I'd just finished writing and demanded the second half. The publicity director asked for a quote. He said, "It reads itself." Now that's a pretty highbrow expression and a few people asked me what it meant!

If the *New York Times* reviewer says, "I promise you that the story will grip you from start to finish," that's fine. But the same quote from a minor source might not work. Some of the weakest blurbs I've seen on books are short quotes from other writers, especially those who write in a genre different from the book they are trying to promote. Some writers trade quotes with other writers, and sophisticated readers do catch on.

The quote that sounds original can have far more impact than the usual adjectives. My all-time favorite quote actually came from a news story rather than a review. A *New York Times* reporter wrote, "If you bury yourself in a Sol Stein book while walking, you'll walk into a wall." P.S. He did.

Reviving Authors

Some days the world seems to be motivated solely by "What's new?" New objects age and become familiar. Today's new becomes old, and revivals happen. Even authors can have a new life with a little thought. A pseudonymous author of commercial books had published twenty-four thrillers when I met him. He got about $10,000 advance for each book and perhaps a bit more when paperback rights were sold, but his income was pretty much the same for each new book. About the time I met him, his most recent book was bought for the movies and the film was a big success. My problem was how to make this event work for the author's new book. In publishing his next book and the first one under our flag I set up an ad that had two columns and two faces, one with his former pseudonym and the other with his "real name." It was an intriguing ad. The regulars bought his new book but so did a far greater number of new readers who'd seen the movie or just succumbed to the ads and the ballyhoo. The author's advances went up to six figures, paperback rights eventually went up to three-quarters of a million dollars, and he kept on writing his books for his new, much larger audience. Just to clarify my position, I revived another author who was not prolific, in fact had only one novel worth republishing, but it won him the Nobel Prize.

Royalties

For books the royalties used to be relatively standard. A new book writer would receive a 10-percent-of-list-price royalty on, say, the first five thousand copies, 12.5 percent on the next five thousand copies, and 15 percent thereafter. A very successful author might get a 15 percent royalty from the outset. One touchy area for a writer and his agent is the royalty on books sold for high discounts, usually to warehouse stores, chains, and other high-volume book retailers. The royalty gets considerably smaller for books sold at high discounts, and this needs to be carefully looked at by the author's agent. If the book in question is highly specialized and unlikely to be a big item for discount outlets, the point is moot. As of this writing, many authors know little about the value of, for instance, electronic rights. The increased complexity of contracts supports the need of working through experienced agents. Also, if an agent has successfully negotiated a particular right or royalty in the past on another author's book, it is sometimes easier for the agent to have that become a standard even for newer authors in the same shop.

Writing or editing books can be surprisingly rewarding if one takes the long view. A contract for a nonfiction book that has a long life can have an originally unimagined value. Very early in my career I had an opportunity to edit two books as a freelancer. One required quite a lot of work, the other almost none. My contract called for a 5 percent royalty that did not come out of the author's share. One of the books was chosen as one of the one hundred best nonfiction books of the twentieth century. The second book, a specialized academic work, saw its sales grow with the years to my surprise (two hundred thousand copies at this writing), and both books have paid royalties both to the authors and to me for more than half a century.

S

Sales Meetings

Publishers tend to have fewer seasons than laypeople because each season requires a catalog of forthcoming books and a sales meeting that brings the salespeople together with the staff that knows the books. The customary meeting may last for several days. Its main purpose other than nighttime partying is the presentation of the new list—that is, the books the salespeople will be offering booksellers that will be published in the forthcoming season. Traditionally editors would be invited to attend and, in as few words as they could manage, to convey information about the books they worked on. Today editors rarely attend sales meetings. The lead books usually get much more attention than their fellows.

At these meetings salesmen are provided with kits containing the forthcoming catalog and promotional materials for the lead books as well as reading copies for the most exalted. Salespersons are known to sometimes deride views contrary to theirs about the market for or salability of some of the titles. In recent years, there has been a trend in which senior financial or administrative executives loom over the meeting and restrain—or not—the impulse of salesmen to put their two cents in. The editorial folks speak from their experience with similar books, but management is management and often feared by the presenters.

For new books that are not "major," salespersons, when calling on bookstore buyers, usually have only thirty seconds per title to say title, author, and one sentence regarding what the book is about, and to mention any promotion that is planned. With lists that take two hours, that's hard to do and still keep boredom at bay. Since the task is nearly impossible, salesmen are known to skip titles—that is, not even mention them to booksellers—and take it for granted that the advance order from that bookseller will be zero. Hence salespeople can help make or break the future of individual titles.

Seasons in Publishing

The seasons of the year and seasons in publishing differ. In publishing, seasons refer to the official release date of a list of new books. Publishers have two or three seasons. Sales meetings at which future publications are described and touted (often by editors who worked on the books) occur well ahead of the season, allowing time for salespeople to read bound galleys of the more important books and study the promotional literature and sales points of each book as well as the track record of the author, especially if it is exceptional. Sometimes one or more authors, especially if famous or experienced and charismatic, will be invited to address the sales staff and mingle with the salespeople. Salespeople like to be able to rest a new book on the record of a preceding book or books.

Self-Publishing

Is it a threat to the commercial publishing house? Not really. Authors would clearly prefer to have their work published by strong commercial firms with prestige, publicity clout, and strong distribution channels. From the publisher's point of view, self-publishing has opened up print on demand as an accessory business. Such a trend would take some of the risk out of publishing, eliminate returns, and be an economical way of serving reader demand. It is also possible that in the not too distant future, print-on-demand facilities will be available in cities everywhere, and the present cost of shipping tons of books will decrease greatly. Moreover, keeping books in print would not be a matter of warehousing inventory. The printing of books would respond to demand.

Stunts Sell Books

Many writers are tactful, considerate human beings. They would never do some of the things I've done to sell books. For instance, I was a guest on David Frost's TV show when *The Magician* came out. The show was done before a packed audience in New York, which almost always has a large contingent of tourists, so at one point I pointed at the studio audience and asked a question: "How many of you have heard of extortion rackets in your local high school?" Amazingly a multitude of hands went up instantly, and we were off and running because the novel I was promoting was about that subject and Frost let me run with that ball. Important point: *The David Frost Show* was syndicated, that is, licensed to other TV stations around the country, so the publicity people at my publishers could alert booksellers to what would appear on the show in their communities. Yes, it takes a bit of audacity to do these things.

The novel that followed was *Living Room*. It begins with the heroine, Shirley Hartman, on the roof of her apartment building contemplating jumping off. That didn't lend itself to what I was willing to do in front of a live audience, so on my tour, right after I was introduced to the audience, I held up a copy of *Living Room* and tore it in half (yes, it's possible to do that with a hardcover book). Invariably there were screams and yelps, sometimes from most people in the audience. That led me into a brief talk about how we all feel differently about a book than we feel about most inanimate objects. After the audience calmed down, I told them some things about the book to entice them to buy a copy of *Living Room*.

Subsidiary Rights

In my time in publishing, subsidiary rights were not subsidiary. They provided early sales—and cash—to publishers from the licensing of paperback rights, book club rights, foreign rights, and motion picture rights, and often were the most profitable aspect of publishing, especially for novels and certain categories of nonfiction. When the major publishers set up their own paperback imprints and exploited the paperback rights themselves, the value of those rights became chancier for both author and publisher. The publisher was no longer licensing a right for cash advances. Now the publisher was increasing his risk and sometimes his profit by publishing the paperback edition himself.

Licensing chapters or parts of a forthcoming book to periodicals is doubly valuable; it provides modest income early and serves to promote interest in the book.

Book club rights also used to produce income early for the publisher; but more important, in my experience, was the advertising of the book clubs, which might entice people who didn't join book clubs to buy the publisher's edition.

T

Track Records

Acquisition editors interested in a new manuscript from an author previously published by another firm will want to find out how well the author's previous book sold. If the numbers are good, the editor will happily present the new book to the editorial board. If the track record for the last book is not good and the editor is still attracted to the new book, he may want to find out what happened and why. As the bean-counting environment of publishing increased, numbers began to matter more, taste and experience less. A personal peeve is how easily new numbers override more important numbers. My second novel, *The Magician,* concerned two sixteen-year-olds and was widely adopted in American high schools and had many translations published abroad. In the United States in hardcover and paperback it sold more than a million copies. Nothing that attracted the original reviewers and readers has changed, and the book could easily be relaunched profitably, but that's not how the system works.

U

Unearned Advances
Publishing contracts call for an advance of X dollars, a guaranteed minimum that should be earned back through book sales and subsidiary rights sales. Any part of such an advance or guarantee that is not earned through sales is a loss to the publisher. Theoretically, a publisher will not offer an advance in excess of what can reasonably be earned back—but there are exceptions. In a competitive market where several publishers are vying for the same book, publishers may be willing to guarantee more than they would normally expect to earn back in sales. The key word is "normally." If a book has a

strong chance of being a bestseller, the publisher may base an advance not on what will be returned through sales but on what a blockbuster book can do for the firm's publishing list. A "big" book that makes the bestseller list or suddenly becomes popular for whatever reason can earn benefits for the publisher by drawing the attention of booksellers and reviewers to other books on the list; by generating the goodwill of booksellers; by getting chains and wholesalers that don't stock minor books excited about a big book; and finally, by garnering prestige that will bring other submissions that might not otherwise have come along. Nevertheless, unearned advances are mainly viewed as a drain on a publisher's bottom line.

V

Value of Books
Should a new coffeepot be given as a birthday gift to a friend? He may love his old pot. Flowers don't last. A fancy cake is high in calories. You wouldn't give a carton of cigarettes to a friend whose health you value. One advantage of a book as a gift is that it can be chosen to compliment the recipient. A card isn't needed. The present itself serves as a card. Books are not hidden away in closets but are displayed on bookshelves, and therefore are frequent visual reminders of a gift that brought pleasure to the reader, as well as being visible marks of literacy and class. Books last longer than most gifts, and if chosen well they increase in value as they age.

W

Warning to New Senior Executives

If you didn't matriculate in the book world but came to publishing because of your executive or economic training and experience, a word to the wise. Let's presume that you read books that were not schoolbooks, and that later you read certain kinds of books that you liked. It's easy to make the error of assuming that the firm you're now in or running ought to publish more books of the kind that you liked to read in your adult years. That's a dangerous assumption because there are indeed many kinds of books, ranging from comic books to literature, and what you may need to do is put your earlier preferences in reading in the closet while you look carefully at what the company you're now helping to steer is good at. It would be a mistake to suggest that Farrar, Straus and Giroux should be doing lots of thrillers and should develop titles in math and economics designed for businessmen. If you wanted a son and your spouse produced a daughter, you would be careful about raising her as a boy. Even the largest publishing conglomerates have subcompanies or imprints that do well with a particular kind of book, and that is what should be improved or nourished with your executive skills.

Writers' Rights

First the bad news. In Europe authors' rights to their own material exist under law. These rights are usually referred to as "the moral right of authors" to use their own writing if it is no longer being used by the publisher and the book is out of print. In the United States, most publishers are good guys and behave honorably; they will revert the rights to authors if books are out of print in the publisher's edition(s) and in subsidiary rights licensee editions. But beware licenses granted for film rights of novels or stories. The licenser will assert ownership of the film rights even if the movie is never made. Moreover, the film studios and producers claim the character rights, meaning that you can't use those character names in any new material. To some writers, including me, it feels like a child of yours has been kidnapped for life.

The best place for the writer to go if he feels that his rights are being abused is the legal department of the Authors Guild, which won't charge for advising you if you are a member. Membership is available to anyone who has had two books published (not self-published) by standard publishers. If you are accepted there is a dues requirement geared to your writing—and only your writing—income. The guild also helps writers who have reached a time and an age when they are no longer able to support themselves. The organization is worth its dues and more for the advice it provides in its quarterly publication and in reviewing contracts.

Essentials for your collection

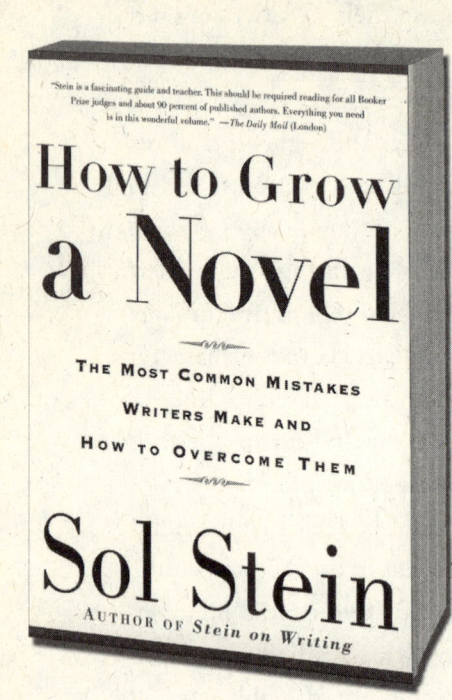

How to Grow a Novel
THE MOST COMMON MISTAKES WRITERS MAKE AND HOW TO OVERCOME THEM
Sol Stein
AUTHOR OF *Stein on Writing*

"Stein is a fascinating guide and teacher. This should be required reading [for] 90 percent of published authors... WONDERFUL."
—*The Daily Mail* (London)

"This book can jump-start anyone's creativity. Highly recommended for all writing collections."
—*Library Journal*

Stein on Writing
A MASTER EDITOR OF SOME OF THE MOST SUCCESSFUL WRITERS OF OUR CENTURY SHARES HIS CRAFT TECHNIQUES AND STRATEGIES
Sol Stein
Author of *How to Grow a Novel*

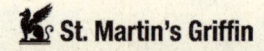

St. Martin's Griffin